Children First

ABCs of School Success—A Guide for Parents

Shirley Babilya Dickinson

The Scarecrow Press, Inc.
A Scarecrow Education Book
Lanham, Maryland, and London
2001

SCARECROW PRESS, INC.
SCARECROW EDUCATION

Published in the United States of America
by Scarecrow Press, Inc.
4720 Boston Way
Lanham, Maryland 20706
www.scarecrowpress.com

Copyright © 2001 by Shirley Babilya Dickinson

British Library Cataloguing-in-Publication Information Available

Library of Congress Cataloging-in-Publication Data
Dickinson, Shirley Babilya, 1961–
    Children first: ABCs of school success : a guide for parents / Shirley Babilya
    Dickinson
        p. cm. (A Scarecrow education book)
    Includes bibliographical references.
    ISBN 0-8108-4020-0 (pbk. : alk. paper)
     1. Education—Parent participation—United States—Handbooks, manuals, etc. 2.
  Home and school—United States—Handbooks, manuals, etc. I. Title. II. Series.
LB1048.5 .D53 2001
372.19'2—dc21   Library of Congress Control Number 2001020064

♾™ The paper used in this publication meets the minimum requirements
of American National Standard for Information Sciences—Permanence of Paper for
Printed Library Materials, ANSI/NISO Z39.48-1992.
Manufactured in the United States of America.

I would like to thank God for my wonderful family, a lifetime of blessings, and this chance to share information to help children succeed in school. I wish to dedicate this book to families with school-age children and especially to my family: to my wonderful son for his love, hugs, and smiles; to my magnificent husband for his support and encouragement; to my loving parents and sisters for their continued belief in me.

Contents

Introduction

America's leaders say that they want higher academic standards and achievement from students in our schools. Parents support this view. Everyone wants their child to go to school in a safe place, focused on teaching and learning. Unfortunately, we also must teach our children how to deal with issues of the twenty-first century. School communities inherit the same social problems that are seen in communities they serve. When looking at a child's school, parents should first look at the community in which they live. We have all seen the many schools around the country plagued with violence. Within the last two years, our country has mourned with our youth after the school shootings at Columbine, Jonesboro, and Edinboro. The 1998 National Report on School Safety indicates that more government monies are being spent on nonviolent conflict resolution, weapon retrieval, drug-free, and survival skills programs in America's schools. School survival and school success has become a primary goal for parents of school-age children.

Many parents wonder about schools and want to know what is going on inside their child's school. This book will provide parents with helpful hints to resolve concerns, prevent violence, and strengthen academics, from kindergarten through high school graduation. As a principal for the last seven years and a teacher for eight years before that, I have had an opportunity to see what is going on from the inside. Parents are on the outside looking in, and I hope to provide practical tips on what to look for and how best to help their children.

Anticipate Reading!

Learning to read is the single most important skill needed to ensure school success. Once children can learn to read independently, they have the key to unlock other academic subjects. Children will be asked to read math word problems, science experiments, and social studies and health books. They will be expected to read and know the rules of the school. Not knowing how to read could put your child in many dangerous situations at school. What would happen to a child who did not learn to read and was given a note from his mom saying that he was not to go home after school but should go to the baby-sitter's house instead? Would the child remember what to do, or would he need to rely on someone to read his note for him? What if a bully read the note and told him the wrong thing and the child went home instead to an empty house because his mom was working late? Reading at an early age can help prevent such situations.

Reading can also save a child's life. Children need to learn to read warning signs in the world around them. What would happen to a child who entered an abandoned coal mine or warehouse because he/she could not read the "Keep Out" sign?

Parents should read to their children when they are young. Toddlers can be shown and read to with heavy board-type books. Preschoolers can listen to their parents read easy books, over and over to encourage word recognition, while school-age children should be encouraged to read independently to themselves or their parents. Parents and children can also share a book by the parent reading the first page out loud, the child reading the second, and so on. Find books that your child will be interested in, or get their teachers to send some books home. You can even make books by drawing pictures to match words, or you can ask your children to tell about their day and make it into a simple book.

Singing songs is another fun way to encourage children to read. You can sing the song, teach your child the words to memorize, and then show her the words in print that go along with the song. This approach is similar to the songs on television that featured a bouncing ball following the words. Children associate music and singing with sounds, and they can easily make the transition of singing those songs to words. You might feel that they are just memorizing the words, but children will begin to recognize these routine words in other forms of print.

Things you do every day can also be made into a learning activity. For example, you can read road signs or point out billboard signs as you travel. Reading ingredients on foods can help children recognize key words. Movie theaters also have a lot of signs posted. Common words such as *popcorn, soda, nachos,* and *cheese* will be of particular interest to your child, since the theater also stimulates other senses, such as smell and taste. You also want your children to be aware of certain signs to help them in everyday life. Some signs are very important to their emotional well-being, and we must teach them to recognize and read these words. For example: you do not want your little girl walking into the men's rest room or your little boy walking into the women's rest room. We must teach our children at an early age that certain signs mean "keep out."

Many parents and children spend much time traveling to the babysitter, to work, to school, or back home again. This travel time can be used to strengthen both reading and math skills. Multiplication tables are best achieved when repeated in the car. Before you leave on a car ride, ask your child a couple of questions regarding signs to look for on the way. You may want to pick up certain cartoons from the newspaper to have your children read while riding (if they do not get motion sickness). Before you leave on a trip, plan to play something like the alphabet game. In our family, we begin like this: "I'm going on a trip and I am going to take an alligator." The second person says, "I'm going on a trip and I am going to take an alligator and a baseball." And so it goes, down the alphabet. This is a good exercise of alphabetical order and memorization. It can be played with two or more players and is a lot of fun. You can help each other to remember or to think of ideas that go with the particular alphabet letter. Finally, the last step of the game should go something like this: "I'm going on a trip and I am going to take an alligator, baseball, cat, Don, Egor, Fred, giraffe, hard hat, ice cream, juggler, king, lion, monkey, nut, orange, penguin, queen, rooster, Shirley, tumbler, umbrella, violin, walrus, X-ray machine, yak, and zebra." There are many games like this one, that can help children and adults to sharpen their skills.

Have a set of magnetic alphabet letters for the refrigerator. These can be a fun source of togetherness while cooking in the kitchen. Have your child pick a letter to start the word, and then you finish it, putting the letters together to make a word. Remember to take turns. Oh, what fun you can have putting words together!

If you must leave for work before your child awakens, then you can leave a note for her to read. Remember to include pictures with the words for beginners. Draw a smiley face near the sentence "You make me so happy." Draw a smiling sun near the sentence "It is going to be a sunny day." These notes can be left at home or sent to a day care provider in your child's pocket or lunch box. School-age children enjoy getting notes in their lunches. This is a fun way to encourage your child to value the importance of reading. Reading is communication.

Always watch for an opportunity to read. Continue to share reading with your children, even after they can read independently. This allows them to enjoy stories that require adult reading skills or that are too difficult to read alone. You may want to read magazines, newspapers, comic strips, and comic books. Subscribe to a favorite children's magazine to arrive in your mailbox. You and your child can anticipate its arrival and reading it each month. You might even want to try a family night out at the local library. A personal library card can place a higher value on reading. A collection of books at home will also encourage reading. Allow your child to choose selections that are of most interest to him. Books with rhymes and poetry provide the perfect blend of reading and speaking practice. These are sometimes the most fun to read.

Educational experts agree that reading aloud to your child is the best way to build a love for reading. Animate the story as you go. It does not have to be perfect; it just needs to be fun. Your child will enjoy good books with humor and funny situations. Find time to read aloud when you are not hurried or stressed for time. Try to choose a book that you both will like. While you read, look for meaning in the story. Ask, "What's happening on this page?" Once you are finished with the story, ask about the characters and things that happened to them in the story. These talks will help your child understand what's going on in the details of the story. Look for new vocabulary words on the written page. Point them out to your child and talk about their meaning. Example: "The little girl was confused. Have you even been confused?" When your child first reads aloud, encourage her to read slowly. It is better to read slowly, pausing to answer your child's questions and discussing the story. You may want to stop in the middle and talk about the way the book is going to end. Example: "What do you think will happen? Will she find her lost roller skates? If she doesn't find them, how will she skate?" Drawing pictures about the story will also help build understanding.

Many schools have programs—during and after school, on weekends, and over the summer—that will help your child become a strong independent reader by the third grade. The programs during the school day include their regular reading instruction, with some type of remediation program available to slow readers. The after-school programs are usually offered in the school library. If your school does not offer such an activity, check with the office to see whether any teachers or older students might be willing to help after school. Weekend programs are an extension of the learning week. If a child has not obtained the academic skills that were expected during the week, some schools offer the assistance of a certified teacher at school on Saturdays. This program is rare, but by encouraging it to be made available, you could make a difference in your child's school. Another type of reading program extends the learning year into the summer, an increasingly popular approach around the country. These programs are funded locally or by state monies, to strengthen and reinforce reading and other skills.

No matter what school program children are enrolled in, they will benefit by becoming stronger readers. The more exposure to and practice with reading children have, the better readers they will become.

Beware of Bullies

The bully in your child's life could be someone in his own class or in another class. The bully could be riding your child's bus. A bully may refuse to allow your child to sit with her friend and push her when she gets on the bus, making the bus ride to school a thoroughly unpleasant experience for your child. During recess, a bully may push extra hard when playing tag or may challenge children to fight daily. Bullies are most often seen on the playgrounds and in the rest rooms, or during unsupervised times of the school day.

As adults, we do not tolerate this type of physical contact in our working environment. Children should not be expected to brush it off, either, since school is the place that they go to "work." As a parent, you cannot always go to school with your child. You must ease your child's fears, while listening to him to gather information. Talk to your children, and probe gently with questions when you notice a fear of school developing. A bully should never be ignored. Bullies gain power with time, and with each victory.

A structured school will help to minimize the effects of bullies. As a parent, you must report a bully to your child's teacher; if the bullying continues, report it to the principal. If the bully cannot be stopped by school officials, then the legal authorities can be contacted to help your child. Little bullies may have parents who react to your efforts by manipulation or bullying themselves. You do not want to try to resolve this difficulty alone. The school officer, local magistrate, and juvenile probation officer can offer legal assistance. Fines or a period of probation with community service to help reform a bully can protect your child from abuse.

Most school districts are required by law to enforce policies that protect children from unlawful harassment and/or bullying. The discipline policy should address inappropriate physical contact, along with other areas such as:

endangering self or others;
disorderly conduct at school or school-related activities;
minor destruction;
indecent conduct;
defiance of authority;
participating in civil acts of disobedience;
disruptive behavior;
verbal and/or physical assault of others;
extortion/making threats;
possession of tobacco, drugs, and alcohol products;
false fire alarm;
bomb scare;
possession of explosives; and
possession of weapons.

If your child is being called names and it impedes her ability to learn at school, school policy would regard this behavior as verbal assault or unlawful harassment. Another, even more serious example of bullying may take the form of drug dealers pressuring your child to buy drugs. Drug possession on school property is a violation of local, state, and federal laws. You have many tools at your disposal in this situation, and many different agencies will listen and *act* on your concerns. A third example may be routine teasing that has escalated to extortion of your child's lunch money. In most cases, extortion is a violation of school policy and the law. If your child's school policy does not address this case, local and state laws do.

School and other policies and laws continue to govern activities/events occurring off school property. If your child rides the bus and the bully is on the bus, school officials should be able to help. If your child is approached by a bully at a school dance on Friday night, the school officials should be able to help with this also. Remember that your child may not wish for you to get involved. If you sense that your child is afraid, tell the authorities this as well. Children are not always able to assess the situation as well as their parents do. We must get involved to help keep our schools a safe place to learn.

The victim may become the aggressor, if left unattended, which makes a parent's job even more difficult when dealing with school officials. Parents often tell their children to stand up for themselves, and children interpret this advice to mean "hit back." The same rules, regulations, policies, and laws that protect us are actively enforced on the bullies. As a parent, we must intervene before our children resort to retaliation and violence. Encourage children to resolve conflicts in nonviolent ways, and be ready to help them with this goal.

Conflict resolution skills are often learned too late. Children need guidance to resolve issues *before* they have serious consequences. Many schools offer conflict resolution programs within their counseling department. These services are available through the office and are directed specifically toward nonviolent resolutions to young people's issues. For more information and additional support, contact one of the following organizations:

- Children's Creative Response to Conflict (CCRC) provides workshops and activities specially designed for participants to experience ways to examine conflict and develop solutions. Write Box 271, 532 N. Broadway, Nyack, NY 19060; phone (914) 358-4601.
- Consortium of Peace Research, Education, and Development (CO-PRED) is devoted to networking, catalyzing, and serving persons or institutions interested in scientific study, action, research, and education on problems of peaceful social change and conflict resolution. Contact c/o Center for Conflict Resolution, George Mason University, 4400 University Drive, Fairfax, VA 22030; phone (703) 273-4485.
- Global Learning offers workshops on global issues for schools, teachers, and parents, with a focus on conflict resolution, world hunger, and international relations. Write 1018 Stuyvesant Avenue, Union, NJ 07083; phone (908) 964-1114.
- Grace Contrino Abrams Peace Education Foundation, Inc., produces peace education and conflict resolution material, including audiovisual media, for kindergarten through twelfth grade. Write 2627 Biscayne Blvd., Miami, FL 33137-4532; phone (305) 576-5075.

- Kids to Kids International has a picture book program in which books created by American children are sent to children around the world. Small packets of drawing supplies are included with each shipment, enabling those receiving the gift to be a giver as well and create a book for others. Free information is available upon request. Write 1961 Commerce Street, Yorktown Heights, NY 10598; phone (914) 243-0305.
- Resolving Conflict Creatively Program promotes effective instruction in creative conflict resolution and intergroup activities. Write 163 Third Avenue, #239, New York, NY 10003; phone (212) 260-6290.
- The Conflict Center is a peace organization with resources and training available on conflict resolution. Write 2626 Osceola, Denver, CO 80212; phone (303) 433-4983.

Choosing the Teacher

All children usually meet one difficult teacher whose personality does not match their own. In this case, a parent can generally head off problems by meeting the teacher *before* serious problems begin. Too often, we wait until the need arises, yet teachers are impressed with parents who get to know their child's teacher. Even if your child is a straight A student, meeting the teacher and principal will help to open lines of communication between you and your child's school. Do it early, and do it now!

Schools should have an open door policy, so that parents can visit their child's classroom at a moment's notice. As a parent, you will want to be sure that practices used would be acceptable for times when you are (and are not) present. Teachers are held to the highest level of expectations because they have one of the most important jobs to do. The children of today will be our leaders of tomorrow. Children are the customers of the schools.

We all know who the best teachers are. All you need to do is to ask your child or some older children in the same school system, and they will readily tell you. We have all heard the horror stories about a few weak teachers, and it seems that they are target for much criticism in today's media world. Some teachers do the minimum of what is expected of them. Teachers should not ridicule or physically strike a child in any way. The mediocre teacher will show signs of instability, and your child will share these stories with you. Listen to your child, and respond in a reassuring manner.

If your child continues to have anxiety over a particular teacher, ask your pediatrician to write a note for your youngster to be switched to a different classroom. Schools are expected to protect the health, safety, and welfare of their students. A doctor's note is very influential in a school system.

Follow a school system's chain of command. The principal is the building manager and instruction leader and, as such, should be your first contact in addressing this issue. Often, he or she will have the authority to make necessary changes in the school. Some teacher contracts, however, prohibit parents from requesting specific teachers, due to the potential damage to weak teachers' professional reputation. You can still push forward with your request by going directly to the director of instruction or the superintendent. The superintendent of schools is the chief officer of the school district and usually has the authority to make changes with very little repercussion. The superintendent also has to answer to the members of the local school board of directors. Make your initial request to meet in writing and send the letter by certified mail to the superintendent's office. You should make your request to choose a teacher early in the summer—May or June—before school starts for the next year.

Usually, the school board, who typically meet once a month, will simply direct school personnel to accommodate such a request once they receive it from the superintendent in writing. They are very busy with important school business. Be sure that they realize that your child's educational assignment is equally important business to you and to your child.

If you still do not receive satisfaction, then you have several options. Private schools offer educational choices and charge tuition. Some parents opt to home-school their children. Current federal legislation is considering parents' options in choosing their children's school. You may want to stay up-to-date with changes that directly impact your right to choose schools.

If all else fails and you simply cannot send your child to the public school in the area, you may want to consider an on-line school. "CyberSchool" opened in Midland, Pennsylvania, for 262 students during the 2000–01 school year. These students picked up their computer, printer, and video equipment for interactive electronic learning from home. There are many CyberSchool links for interested parents to find more information. Here are a few to get you started:

http://www.midlandpa.org/wpccs/
http://www.susqcyber.org/
http://www.thepittsburghchannel.com/pit/news/stories/
    news-20000924-150802.html
http://www.lancaster.k12.pa.us/CyberSchoolIntel.htm
http://www.insightmag.com/archive/200006124.shtml
http://www.dispatch.co.za/2001/01/01/features/CYBER.HTM
http://abcnews.go.com/sections/scitech/DailyNews/
    onlineed001228.html

Discipline Dos and Don'ts

At the beginning of the year, schools generally send out a student handbook clearly outlining their discipline policy. You will want to know what options are available to be inflicted on your child, *before* something happens. Parents sometimes disagree with the discipline in their child's school. For example, if you don't want your child paddled, write a note to the principal forbidding the child to receive corporal punishment.

Read the handbook with your child, so that she understands the consequences of her actions. The school is a community where people have rights. Children get in trouble when their actions infringe directly on the health, safety, and welfare of others. It is important as a parent that you get all the facts before becoming enraged at either your child or the school.

Often, parents look for a way out of problems for their child at an early age, because they find it hard to believe that their child is in trouble. This approach only magnifies their problems later in life as the child matures and perhaps gets involved in bigger, more serious infractions. Consider this example: How would a person in a grocery store react to your pushing him out of the way to pass at the checkout cashier? Would he be understanding if you took a bite out of his food, as it was being paid for? Would you expect to get away with hitting the check-out clerk, because she was not doing what you wanted her to do? We must help our children to take small steps, especially when they make mistakes.

Children need to understand that school is filled with choices and consequences, just as life is. We have to support the choices they make and also follow through with consequences to teach them right from wrong! If your child makes an incorrect choice and gets in trouble, it is very important for you to become directly involved. When the school personnel (teachers or principal) contact you, they will do so by phone, by mail, or through a note sent home with your child. Teachers will generally contact you for minor infractions, while the principal's call means serious business. Discipline conferences can range from a parent conference, after-school detention, in-school suspension, to out-of-school suspension depending on the nature and seriousness of each incident. Each consequence should be mentioned in the student handbook and can be reviewed for appropriateness to your child's current problem.

It is better to be proactive rather than reactive in dealing with school personnel. If you have questions about the discipline policy, it is best to ask before a personal conflict arises.

Conflict resolution is a new tool in a bag of tricks that seems to defuse problems with children, before they escalate to violence. The term *conflict resolution* is not new to education, yet only recently have we seen conflict resolution programs emerge. The rash of violence in schools throughout the country has prompted educators, administrators, and parents to work together to solve some of the issues that face young people today. Ask your child's school counselor or principal about conflict resolution programs offered in the school.

Talk to your child and give him examples of conflicts that you as a child experienced. Talk about how you resolved crises and how you would wish your child to resolve issues. Times have changed, but one thing stands true: children continue to need the guidance of their parents. If you listen and guide them rather than criticize them, you will play a very active part of these skills in your child. You may want to listen to what he has to say and help him devise his own plan (with your guidance) so that your child learns how to resolve, problem-solve, and overcome minor obstacles, evolving toward a productive adulthood.

Remember that children need to know the rules to follow them. Exceptions to the rules are confusing to children. They do not understand exceptions to the rule. Family rules, like class rules, should apply to everyone in the group. Discuss consequences ahead of time for when a rule is broken; children need to know the consequences up front.

Children need to feel loved—even when disciplined. Make the discipline reasonable and consistent. For example, "You are grounded until you get married" is unrealistic for a consequence. We all know that a child cannot be grounded for her entire life. "You are to clean your room before you go out" is more reasonable for a child. Rules and consequences need to change, as the child grows. Adjust your discipline consequences to be age-appropriate for your children, as they mature.

Exceptional Students

Parents with children who have disabilities or disorders such as attention deficit/hyperactivity disorder (ADHD) have different challenges than the parent of a child without these exceptionalities. Our federal and state governments have set regulations and guidelines to help all children to succeed in school. Parents should learn how to write a contract with their school district and prepare to meet with the team of school professionals, to help their child receive special services while learning. The next few pages will help. Also refer to the chapter on learning disabilities for more help from agencies and documents available to parents who wish to find additional information.

- *Don't be afraid of your child's multidisplinary evaluation (MDE) team.* The most important person on the multidisciplinary team is you—the parent. The principal, teachers, psychologist, counselor, nurse, physical therapist, occupational therapist, and so forth, all can be additional members of your child's team. You even have the right to request that your own pediatrician, therapist, counselor, and/or attorney be included as a member of the decision-making team. This team reviews all the information on your child and together formulates a proposal to help your child's individual needs. This team makes the recommendations to the IEP (individualized education plan) team. If you do not agree with the team, you have the most authority. As in the voting process, you have the powerful right to veto or disagree! It is always best to keep an open mind, and listen to the members of the team and to what they are saying in the best interest of your child.

- *What does an IEP look like?* The IEP begins with basic information from the parents, teachers, principal, and even the school counselor and psychologist. This section mentions your child's strengths and what she enjoys most. It then continues to identify the data (i.e., test results, observations, classroom performance, medical needs) that will help determine whether your child has a learning disability. In later pages, you will see the educational goals and how the school plans to meet your child's individualized educational needs. The IEP is similar to a signed contract with the school, which is legally held responsible to carry out the goals and objectives for the student. Be sure that all members have signed this document to indicate their participation, and keep a copy in a very safe place—if you should ever need to enforce it!

- *How to write a contract for special services in the school.* A contract for special services in Pennsylvania is called a 504 Agreement of Services. Other states may have a different name, but nationally the idea is still the same. This is a contract for children who have a hidden disability or a medical condition not covered in the special education regulations, but who still need extra support to succeed at school. These agreements can be short, describing the role of a personal care aide, or long, delineating the different supports throughout the school day (adaptive physical education, quiet lunch, play therapy, etc.).

- *There are people who can help.* If you meet with resistance or as a parent you feel intimidated by school officials, people are available to serve as your advocate. Many different agencies have child advocates, and your local Children and Youth Services office may be able to point you in the right direction. Advocates are helpful because they know the law, and they know *your child's rights.* A child with special needs may not be able to succeed without some modifications of her educational day, and advocates can make special recommendations, such as the enlargement of all worksheets so your child can read them more easily. Some children need a specially equipped van for transportation, while others need special tools to work with in class. All of these areas can help facilitate a positive learning environment for the child, and modifications will vary depending on need.

- *Support groups* can be located worldwide on the Internet and locally in your telephone directory. It is often a good idea to connect with parents in your similar situation, to support each other and learn from one another's mistakes. As they say, we don't need to reinvent the wheel; we don't need to stumble alone in the dark. Together parents can accomplish twice as much. Accept help from agencies and other parents. Many of these people can become like friends to you and your family. They are available to support children and so you already have something in common to talk about.

- *The federal Individuals with Disabilities Education Act Amendments of 1999* (PL 105-17), commonly referred to as "IDEA 99," require school districts to provide free and appropriate public education (FAPE) to all students with disabilities who are eligible for special education. FAPE means special education and related services are designed to meet the individual educational needs of your child. These services must be described in an IEP and provided to you at no cost. You also have the right under federal law to file a complaint with the Department of Education of your state and/or to begin due process procedures for an informal hearing, mediation, due process hearing, and so forth, if large problems arise. If you cannot agree with school officials, these options provide an opportunity to resolve problems without going directly to the courts. The United States Department of Education, Special Education Programs Office, can offer you additional assistance and detailed information to address your own personal needs.

Empower yourself to support your child. The school districts, Department of Education, advocacy agencies, and support groups exist to take good care of children. Don't be afraid to ask for help. They are in the business to help.

Family, Fun, and Field Trips

Many schools provide a well-rounded menu of educational experiences, but schooling in the twenty-first century should be fun as well. Children benefit when they learn while having fun. If they are afraid, they will not receive the full benefit of preparedness for life. Each child should enjoy going to school and look forward to the fun they will have there.

Many times of the school day are fun. If your school offers a breakfast program, this is generally a fun, talkative time for youngsters. They can meet with their friends and enjoy a healthy breakfast at the same time. Other fun times include lunch and recess. Parents want to be sure to take full advantage of meal programs, and some children may even qualify for government-sponsored (free and reduced) food programs at school. Regardless of your finances, your child should be able to have fun and food during these times at school.

Classroom time also should include fun-enhancing participation in learning activities. Children learn best by doing things and should be actively engaged in learning throughout most of the school day. Good teachers include thematic units and multisensory approaches to learning that involve cut-and-paste artwork, performance, listening, free reading, and even daydreaming in everyday lessons. A schoolwide theme may include food, dress, crafts, songs, movies, and academic lessons on a particular topic.

Field trips are fun. Most schools now participate in annual field trips for each grade level. Parents can go along as chaperones and enjoy the educational day with their child. Kindergarten may go to the Children's

Museum for a day, while the sixth grade may go to Washington, D.C., for three days. Some schools have Rewards Day Trips, to reward and encourage children with good behavior. These may range from an afternoon of bowling with classmates, to a teddy bear picnic at the local park.

Assemblies, pep rallies, and puppet shows also add fun to the school day. Assemblies are often hosted by local theater groups, grant awards, or companies that have a theme or message. Sometimes they include a lesson about drug and alcohol awareness or conflict resolution skills. Pep rallies include a strong message of school pride. These types of activities build social and emotional character and develop a sense of belonging in children. Being a student at school means being part of a great team! Puppet shows are good storytellers that include a moral lesson or an academic concept for small children in a friendly way. Many puppet shows address topics such as "Stranger Danger" or "Home Alone" concepts. These programs give children the ideas of how to protect themselves when presented with potentially dangerous situations, without actually scaring them in the learning process. For example, they watch the bunny puppet learn to stay at home alone and see that he should not throw water on a grease fire. They may watch a puppet being led into a stranger's car with the bribery of candy and learn from the puppet's actions to protect themselves. Schools are expected to teach the academics, and much, much more!

School dances are another good way for a parent to become involved in fun at school, by volunteering as a chaperone. This is a great way for parents to see who their child's friends are, what they do, and how they act. As they say, a picture paints a thousand words. In addition, this opportunity is priceless in the development of your child's social and emotional growth.

If your child comes home with a smile, it means the school is providing a wide range of fun educational experiences. Be sure to talk to your children about what they did in school each day. This will give you an opportunity to share in the lessons and to tailor them to your own family's needs, wishes, and expectations. Listen to their explanations about the puppet shows, assemblies, pep rallies, and movies. Be an active participant in your child's learning. Continue to stay involved in your child's life, and reap the rewards in all facets of learning.

Groups and Gangs

Parents in today's world *must* know who their child's friends are! If they don't help to pick their child's friends, someone else will. Kids today are different in many ways. They want a sense of belonging, yet they like to think of themselves as independent at an early age. The trick is for a parent to balance both effectively.

Each child wants to belong to a family unit, and a gang/group will take the place of a family unit. Groups and gangs are in many schools across America. Gang dress and rituals provide a sense of stability and belonging, and gang membership brings respect and a feeling of power that children are attracted to. Recent reports in the media indicate a disturbing trend in gang participation. Gangs are no longer made up of troubled adolescents in poor areas: Gang members are joining at a very young age, and many are from middle-class families.

It may be natural for kids to form groups with like talents and interests. This is normal behavior of interacting with their peers. But when a clique becomes involved in delinquent behavior, it then becomes a gang. Gang activity might begin with thrill-seeking behaviors such as drug abuse or sexual activity and can escalate to spray-painting, vandalism, underage drinking, shoplifting, illegal firearms, rape, and armed robbery.

Everyone wants a gang-free community—except gang members. Parents stand to lose the most when the well-being or the life of their child hinges on a gang activity. Parents must become organized against the gangs in their community. Together they can form a Neighborhood

Watch or community patrol, let the police know of gang activity, and find out what services are available to work against gang involvement in their community. Most importantly, help your child become involved in activities that are directly correlated with the school, charity, sports, church, and other community groups. Idle time may give gangs in the neighborhood a chance to connect with your child.

Most parents do not like to think that their child could become involved in a group that supports violence. The National Association of Elementary School Principals released a *Report to Parents* to offer parents suggestions on how to keep children out of gangs. Here's a summary of its pointers:

1. **Be available**. By forming close and loving relationships with your children while they are young and assuring them that they are valued members of the family, you lessen the risk of alienation once they go into middle and high school.
2. **Know your child's friends**. Encourage your child to invite friends to your home. Supervise your children's activities, and always know where they are and what they are doing.
3. **Be alert to changes in behavior**. Parents know their child best. They know if the child is vulnerable to peer pressure. Sneaking out without permission, receiving lower grades, and wearing different clothing may signal gang involvement. Gang members often display distinctive hairstyles, jewelry, and fingernails. Gangs often communicate with "secret" words, slogans, and hand signals.
4. **Use your child's school as a resource**. Gang recruitment often takes place within the school community since it parallels the local community itself. Administrators are usually aware of any gang activity and problems. Talk to your principal to find out about gangs in your area. Ask the principal about the gang names and their territories, members, and activities. Schools are also good sources of information about ways to resist peer pressure, refuse drugs, solve social problems, and resolve conflicts.

If you think your child may already be in a gang, contact your school principal, nurse, guidance counselor, or law enforcement officer. They can refer you to the appropriate sources of assistance and counseling. The following agencies are also ready and also willing to help:

- Administration of Children, Youth, and Families, (202) 205-8051: extensive information on grant programs that support gang prevention/intervention programs
- Targeted Outreach Program, Boys and Girls Clubs of America, (212) 351-5911: program based in individual clubs that provides outreach to home and family and coordination with the police and other community agencies
- Drugs and Crime Data Center and Clearinghouse, (800) 666-3332: articles, bulletins, reports, updates, and other gang-related information
- National Youth Gang Information Center, (800) 446-4262: helps communities nationwide create practical and effective responses to gang activity
- Bureau of Alcohol, Tobacco, and Firearms, (800) ATF-GUNS: handles reports on illegal activity involving guns
- Police Executive Research Forum, (202) 466-7820: has a variety of publications and background information on how law enforcement agencies can effectively deal with the gang problem
- National Association of Elementary School Principals, (703) 684-3345

In contrast to gang behavior, many activities that your child does with groups of peers are positive in nature. Sports, for example, encourage a sense of belonging to a group focused toward common goals. In many cases, baseball, basketball, volleyball, football, soccer, and golf teams promote positive involvement and belonging. The team celebrates their success as a *team*! Remember, too, that federal laws promote equal access to sports by both genders. School districts are required to have equal representation, whether they be the number of participants on a team or the number of teams.

Sports teams are not the only teams, of course. There are cheerleaders, debate teams, academic quiz bowl teams, bowling leagues, marching band, yearbook and school newspaper staffs, and groups for nearly every hobby imaginable. These teams often require a specific skill that your child can enhance and further develop. Whatever his interests, there is a positive group for your child.

The best action to prevent gang involvement is to become proactive early in your child's life by promoting *positive* group activity. The most difficult choices as a parent come when a reactive decision must be made—when you must react to a situation after your child has gotten in trouble. Try your best to keep your child out of trouble, by reducing the number of reactive decisions you will need to make.

Helping with Homework

The responsibility for completing homework rests with the child, with some prompting from the teacher and parents. Most parents already help with homework. This is an opportunity to bond with your children, no matter what their age. Children enjoy their parents' attention and quality time when working on academics together. This quality time is an investment in your child's future.

Homework calendars can be helpful if your child forgets what homework there is to do or sometimes opts to play first and do homework second. This delay in homework makes it even more difficult to return to the school books. Homework calendars are designed to be a weekly tool to help overcome these troubles. Contact your child's teachers or, if they have already notified you about missing homework, suggest the homework calendar. A tiny spiral notebook, date planner, or sheet of paper with blocks similar to a calendar will work.

Most teachers write the homework on the blackboard. The children then copy the homework subject, pages, and assignment to bring home on that day's page in the calendar. If there is no homework, they should write "no homework" in that subject area. Parents then can ask their children for this sheet of paper when they come home to help with homework. Parents can initial the sheet or date the planner nightly so that the teacher can easily refer to it, if the child misses homework. Ask the teacher to communicate regularly through this homework calendar/planner. You, too, can send the teacher a note that might encourage continuation of a successful venture. Thank the teacher for helping to make your child more responsible and for helping you to teach her study skills that will be useful later in life.

Having an *extra set of books at home* can be useful with a child who is really trying to get out of doing homework. If your child is a repeat offender and often forgets books at school, ask the school if you can take an extra set of books out on loan until the end of the year. You may not need every book—only the subjects that the child routinely avoids. This extra set of books can also help you to review and reteach concepts that your child has difficulty with during the school day. Most parents do not realize that their tax monies pay for the books, which entitles them to seek out ways to work together with the school as educational partners.

As you collect the books, remember to set expectations for the completion of homework. Before each study session, make a mental list of what needs to be done. Then help your child by monitoring her progress, while working on each skill. Organize materials and supplies. Offer positive reinforcement such as "You are really moving ahead!" or "You are finished with two assignments and only have one more to go—nice job!" Review assignments periodically with your child to prevent cramming the night before a test.

The *homework hotline* is a rather new concept available in many different formats. This is a great way to keep track of your child's efforts and upcoming events. Some schools have a phone number that you can call, with an extension number to reach your child's teacher and assignments. The teachers put their assignments (usually for the entire week) in message form on the homework hotline. This helps parents who need to check in after normal school hours. The answering service sometimes provides a voice recording of assignments, as well as an opportunity for parents to leave a message for the teacher.

Now that many homes across America are connected to the *Internet,* the World Wide Web has become a household communication tool as well. Children can communicate with their friends and get on-line with their school to get their homework for the week. If your child has missed school or is forgetful about homework, this may be the solution you have been looking for. Schools post *electronic bulletin boards* and provide a wealth of information for parents at these sites. Some schools also keep track of students' grades via the computer, and parents may monitor their child's progress simply by logging on the information highway.

School Web sites offer information about how you can contact your child's teacher, principal, and other personnel. These sites are usually very general in nature but may contain useful information to refer to when needed, such as the tutoring or reteaching opportunities available. The school Web site may show the school's attendance rate and/or overall performance scale, which may be an indicator of why your child is having difficulty. For example, if a school has an average daily attendance rate of 70 percent, that means that 30 percent of the student population chose to miss school. This figure may indicate that the school is not inviting to children or that they are often ill. If the school's overall performance rating is low, your child may not like the way that learning is presented and may want to skip homework, because he had too many written assignments that day. Information like this and so much more can empower a parent to help a child through school.

A *fax machine* can be a parent's friend. Often if your child gets in trouble for forgetting his homework, you could ask that the assignments be faxed to you at the beginning of the week. Most schools require their teachers to submit lesson plans to the principal—the instructional leader—at the beginning of the week. These plans could be easily faxed to you at home or work. Some schools have a policy about faxing, and you may want to check on the policy provisions to be sure. If the school administrator does not feel comfortable helping you by fax, maybe the secretary could fax them upon receipt in the office.

Generally, teachers themselves do not have access to the fax machines, but instead they could easily copy their plans, provided that you understand they do not follow them verbatim. The process of learning is not something that can be written in a short plan. The plan serves as a guide, and parents should only use it as a guide. Lesson plans can be found on file in the office and with your child's teacher.

The Internet can be a more direct homework helper if used properly and monitored by parents in the home. Parents may want to give their children a chance to visit the following sites, while working with them at the computer to find homework solutions and develop good study habits:

http://www.studyweb.com
http://www.homeworkcentral.com

http://looksmart.com
http://www.komando.com
http://kids.infoplease.com
http://www.infoplease.com
http://www.biography.com
http://www.bjpinchbeck.com
http://www.internetschoolhouse.com
http://www.schoolwork.org
http://www.researchpaper.com
http://www.thepaperboy.com
http://www.all-linkls.com/newscentral
http://www.cliffs.com
http://www.homeworkheaven.com

Investigate Internet Involvement

With the introduction of the Internet into most homes across America, parenting has become even more challenging. It seems as if overnight a whole new window of both opportunity and danger has opened. If your child is not on-line already, he may soon be joining the ten million children who are using the Internet (Find/SVP's 1997 Internet User Survey).

The good news is that the on-line world offers children experiences that are educational and rewarding. Using the Internet effectively as a resource tool may enhance a child's performance and career choices. Your child can research an upcoming vacation spot, listen to audio renditions of famous speeches of history, or view art displayed in European galleries—without leaving the house. There are endless uses of the Internet, with parent involvement and common sense.

Simultaneously, this new technology also can present dangers for children and teens. For example, recently *48 Hours* reported that a young girl in New Hampshire had been stalked on the Internet until her death. Her killer planned her death and put her picture on the Internet before he carried out his plan.

The Internet poses new challenges for parents because, unlike television or radio, the Internet is subject to very few official controls, it has no restrictions on advertising to children, and it is interactive. Your child can interact with strangers from your home, school, or library. The Internet allows anyone, anywhere, to post any information, including materials that are inappropriate and misleading to children. Don't believe everything you see on-line: someone claiming to be a

5'6" brunette female may actually be a 6'2" male. Strangers, at times pretending to be someone else, can communicate directly with your child.

It is important not to overreact if you find out that your child or teen has been talking on-line to a stranger. Talk about what can be done to avoid the same situation the next time. While the chances of a cyber predator showing up at your doorstep are slim, there are cases where they have arranged secret meetings in the "real world."

The concepts of safety and responsibility on the Internet are similar to any other rules: You must become active as your children's first teacher and coach them throughout different periods of their lives. Help them use common sense. If you don't help your children with making responsible choices, someone else may invite them to make irresponsible ones!

Currently, the Computer Crime Unit monitors the Internet, and we can expect anti–cyber stalking laws and Internet privacy laws from the federal government. There are ways to protect children without taking away the adult population's First Amendment rights. As an informed parent, you can help to make the Internet a safer place for your child to learn with a few easy steps:

- Spend time with your children as they search and "chat" on-line, whether at home, at the library, or at school. Your individual attention and support will help children remain focused and away from the hidden dangers.
- Stay informed about the parental tools that will help to watch your child's activity online. Each control tool varies in its determination of whether materials are "inappropriate" or "safe for kids." Filtering devices can be used to block out pornography and other undesirable content from your home. A local store that sells computer software can help you choose one that is right for your family.
- Keep the computer in a family area, so that it is easy to monitor your child's activity informally as family members walk past. Turn the computer so that you and others can easily see the screen often. This low-tech approach could be the best cyber-watch there is!

- Establish strict rules for purchasing products on-line, entering contests, answering surveys, and so forth. These gimmicks are often intended to lure children into giving their names and addresses.
- Contact your Internet service provider if you do find activity on a Web site to be offensive to your family. After all, you are the paying customer, and they want your business. If families generate most of their revenue, they may monitor their own sites more often.
- Enforce the time limits you as parents have set. Children should not be permitted to browse the Web for hours at a time. This permits exploration and extended opportunities to find the hidden secrets not meant for children. Easy access to games may include excessive violence and gender stereotypes.
- Teach your child never to give out personal information such as his name or address, school name or address, or anything else that is personally identifying. Block private messages between the child and another user.

There are no foolproof methods, but there are ways at least to try to find out what your kids are doing on the Internet. If something happens on-line that makes them feel uncomfortable, make sure that they tell you about it right away.

Today, learning to use the Internet is like reading, writing, and arithmetic. It's a basic necessity. The Internet is extremely valuable, but kids need to be streetwise to use the information highway. For more information at an industry-sponsored safety site, visit Getnetwise.org. For a free printed copy of *Child Safety on the Information Highway* or *Teen Safety on the Information Highway,* call the National Center for Missing and Exploited Children at (800) 843-5678.

Jump-Start Learning

Many learning games offer parents and their children a fun way to jump-start learning while in the car or at home. Several schools also have programs that can help, as do the Internet Web sites listed at the end of this section. Here are some skills to work on with a preschooler:

- *Counting to ten.* Your child is anxious and waiting to learn how to count. It's as easy as 1-2-3! At first, your child can memorize the one through ten list of numbers. Next comes counting objects to make the learning more meaningful.
- *Counting objects.* Once a child is interested in numbers, a parent can point and count out loud. Counting objects can range from counting chairs, dinner spoons, toys, or birds flying overhead. This helps a child to better understand the meaning of a number. All of the activities should be visual and at the beginning touchable as well. Cheerios make a good counting tool, along with M&M's and other favorites. Children enjoy these activities, since they can eat the rewards when finished with their counting tools. They can also learn the numerical difference between eating one and eating five Oreo cookies. They can understand that three dogs barking make more noise than one dog barking.
- *Naming colors.* Colors are easy, yet somewhat abstract. Children cannot taste yellow, but they can see it. They cannot hear green, but they can see it. Conversation provides the best opportunity to point out colors and repeat them. Point out to your toddler the yellow school bus, the red apple, the blue carpet, and so forth. Then

begin using crayons to color objects. Coloring may seem simple to an adult, yet it brings hours of relaxation and enjoyment to children. Children will learn more when they are having fun.

- *Reciting the alphabet.* The ABC song makes it easy for children to memorize the alphabet. Saying the alphabet aloud is the first step to learning alphabetical order.

- *Cutting with scissors.* Children need practice cutting with scissors. This requires special skills that educators call *fine motor skills*— those requiring delicate small-muscle activity such as all kinds of handiwork: cutting, coloring, writing, drawing, and so forth. Find blunt-pointed scissors and allow your children to cut along lines or cut pictures or words from magazines and newspapers to practice their cutting skills. When they can use the scissors to cut out specific items, have them cut along straight and finally curved lines. Enjoy and celebrate their success!

- *Drawing a man.* Some IQ tests ask a child to draw a picture of themselves or of a man. Intelligence is then often found in the details of the drawing. For example, if a child draws a man with hair, a hat, a smile, shoes, and buttons on his shirt, this rendition may be considered advanced compared to the basic stick-figure person. Encourage your child to draw what she sees, and point out the things you feel that she missed. Get the child to see the big picture, with the details.

- *Copying a square.* Copying a square is a simple task, yet it is difficult for many toddlers. This activity can prepare your child for copying from the blackboard in school. Once he can copy the square, put a smiley face in the next square to copy, adding an extra step.

- *Printing his name.* Most schools ask that a child can print his first name when entering. A parent can help with this at home. Celebrate the correct way to hold a pencil. Get excited about the proper formation of the letters. Your child's name will be with him for the rest of his life. It is important! It is his identity.

- *Knowing the home address.* Children need to know how to recite—not necessarily write—their address. So often as a principal I've had children tell me that they lived "in the white house next to Grandma" or "in the last house on the street," but they could not give me additional information to help them find their way home on the first day of school. Make sure your child knows her address.

- *Knowing parents' names.* Your child should know your name. Sure, they know you as Mommy or Daddy, but they need to know your full name, in case of an emergency. Be sure that they can recite your name as early as four years old.

- *Understanding opposites (in/out, up/down, etc.).* Opposites are so much fun, and many books provide children with a chance to learn about them. Dr. Seuss books, for example, have lots of fun with these concepts, while including rhyming words.

For more information and additional learning suggestions, browse the following Web sites:

Have fun while learning: http://www.funbrain.com

Easy games: http://www.games.net

Reviews of children's software by kids, parents, and teachers: http://www.superkids.com

Have fun coloring: http://www.crayola.com

The Discovery Channel: http://www.discovery.com or http://www.school.discovery.com

Know the Nurse

The school nurse can help in the case of an injury or if you need someone to administer medication at school. Kids will be kids, and I have seen kids chip a tooth, break a limb, fall from above, experience head injury, and more while at school. Some children also come to school today as juvenile diabetics or with brittle bone disease, cystic fibrosis, muscular dystrophy, hearing aids, or any one of dozens of other medical conditions. This section will explain some of the school's responsibility to children.

- *Vaccinations and exemptions.* Laws govern the number and amounts of vaccinations required before entering school, and these vary from state to state. The school nurse will notify you of the requirements upon entry at school; however, you may want to check on this in advance so that your child does not have to receive a large quantity of immunizations within the summer before school starts. Most states also have state-approved exemptions that include a religious, medical, and philosophical exemption from immunizations/vaccinations. Parents should check with the National Vaccine Information Center in Vienna, Virginia, for more information on exemptions.
- *Administering medications at school.* The school district will usually have a policy either to prohibit administering medication at school or to designate only certain personnel approved to give children their medications. Daily doses, inhalers, treatments, blood level checks, and the like most often will be done by the school nurse. She would then be a key to your child's wellness at school.

In the absence of the nurse, often the secretary or principal is designated as a backup to serve children in need of medicines. Teachers are sometimes designated to give medicines on field trips or in an emergency situation.

- *Emergency planning.* Emergencies can entail a medical crisis, an accident, or early dismissals for severe weather, bomb threats, electricity outage, and more. The school nurse focuses on the health, safety, and welfare of the children and personnel, when making a referral to dismiss school as a safety measure. We can help our children to remain calm by planning and preparing them for the unexpected. For starters, parents need to give the school an alternate contact to call. Working parents usually will provide phone numbers for their place of employment; their cell phone and pager; and their child's grandparents, neighbor, and/or baby-sitter. It is important that you plan for emergencies before they occur in other ways, too. Often the nurse will ask which hospital you prefer in case of a serious emergency, for instance. In the absence of a parent or guardian, the school nurse (together with the doctor) may need to make the necessary decisions in an emergency. In all possible emergency scenarios, it is very important that you are able to be reached during the school day.

- *Allergies and allergic reactions.* Many children today have allergies to many different things that can deter them from learning to their best ability. Parents need to communicate these allergies to the nurse. As the principal, I have made often special arrangements to accommodate children who were allergic to bees, cleaning solvents, milk, peanuts, strawberries, latex, and so forth. Many different accommodations can be made for your child; all you have to do is communicate these allergies first to the nurse first, to the teacher, and finally to the principal.

- *Health and dental screenings.* Health and dental screenings are part of the government's expectations of schools in many states. Laws vary from state to state. In Pennsylvania, for example, children are required to show evidence of healthy teeth and a physical checkup by either their doctor at their own expense or the doctor provided at school for free. This is part of the commitment to securing the health, safety, and welfare of children.

- *Lice, chicken pox, measles, mumps, and other childhood conditions.* Childhood diseases are usually encountered by new parents once their child enters school. Preschoolers who stay at home do not come in contact with a larger number of children until they enter school as a student. This contact increases the chance of acquiring a childhood disease. Lice is included in this category, because usually lice are spread by the sharing of hats, combs, and brushes among students. Lice can become an epidemic if left unnoticed and untreated. Your child can become reinfested with lice once he returns from home to school again. The school nurse should be notified when your child is afflicted by any of the childhood diseases or any other medical need, so that the staff can take precautions of disinfecting desks, door knobs, and other surfaces and checking for symptoms of other students in the room. We all have a stake in the welfare of everyone's children. By helping others, you may actually be helping your own child. The school nurse and principal will appreciate your help.

For more information on health-related issues, visit these Web sites:

http://www.achoo.com
http://www.phys.com
http://www.healthanswers.com
http://www.healthyideas.com
http://www.ama-assn.org
http://www.bottomlinesecrets.com
http://certifieddoctor.org/verify.html
http://www.caloriecontrol.org
http://www.dietitian.com
http://www.rxlist.com
http://www.doctorsoncall.com
http://www.healthfinder.gov
http://www.healthatoz.com
http://www.yourhealth.com

Learning Disabilities

Sometimes in a family one child may get good grades without trying, while another may work hard at studying but still not make the grades. Parents may have difficulty understanding the difference between the learning styles of their children. A number of physical conditions can make learning difficult for a child, including hunger, allergies, or hyperactivity. Continued struggles, however, may indicate that a child has a learning disability.

Learning disabilities are hidden disabilities. Most adults recognize physically challenged individuals, yet parents are frustrated when dealing with their own child's learning disability. We can all understand the need for handicapped parking, a wheelchair ramp, and elevators in schools. We then should also understand the need for small-group instruction, verbal cues, manipulatives, and other learning aids for students with special needs.

These kids do not process information the same way as others do. They cannot be "forced" to learn the same way. It just will not happen, because of their learning disability.

Frequently, bright children have been referred to psychologists or pediatricians because they exhibit certain learning difficulties, speech and language difficulties, and/or certain behaviors (e.g., impulsivity, restlessness, inattentiveness, excessive activity, fidgeting in seat, talking out, daydreaming). Often such characteristics can indicate one of the following learning disabilities:

ADD—attention deficit disorder
ADHD—attention deficit/hyperactivity disorder

CAPD—central auditory processing disorder
Dyslexia—language-based disorder characterized by difficulties in single-word decoding
DAS—dyspraxia-apraxia childhood speech delay
NLD—nonverbal learning disorder

I want to give hope to parents who may be experiencing a hard time with learning in today's schools. Before parents decide to home school their child, they should learn all that they can about their child's own disability. School psychologists can efficiently access children's cognitive skills using a number of well-standardized testing instruments, thereby providing parents with useful information about their child's ability to learn.

Children with *ADHD* may be seen as ADHD at school, but not by the parent, baseball coach, or music teacher. The child's active behaviors exist in all settings but are more of a problem in some settings than others. A parent of an ADHD child may notice the child's high activity level in church or while waiting quietly in a doctor's office, settings similar to the classroom.

An active child who fidgets or misbehaves is often first identified as having ADHD, yet that may not be the case at all. For example, a *gifted child*'s (of superior intelligence) inability to stay on task is likely related to boredom, a slow-paced curriculum, mismatched learning style, or other factors. Gifted children are able to complete work quickly and may spend from 25 to 50 percent of their regular classroom time waiting for others to catch up and finish. This use of extra time in gifted children is often the cause of an improper referral for an ADHD evaluation, since they use this extra time in idle ways. Be careful to know the difference.

A child showing symptoms commonly associated with a true diagnosis of ADHD engages in dangerous physical activity without consideration of the consequences, is more restless than peers, has difficulty playing quietly, has difficulty following directives and multistep directions, squirms in his seat, fidgets with the hands or feet, and has difficulty waiting his turn when playing games.

Formally, the *Diagnostic and Statistical Manual of Mental Disorders* (DSM-III-R) of the American Psychiatric Association lists fourteen characteristics that may be found in children diagnosed as having ADHD. Parents may want to look further into this topic at their local library.

Another common learning disability identified in schools is *dyslexia*. It is a specific language disorder, characterized by difficulties in single-word decoding, that impacts severely on the child's ability to read. In diagnosing dyslexia, a full range of areas must be reviewed. Although decoding skills can be remediated, the exact pattern of symptoms differs in each child. Dyslexia can be a lifelong issue, even after reading skills have developed to an expected level.

The National Vaccine Information Center (NVIC), along with Barbara Loe Fisher, coauthor of *DPT: A Shot in the Dark,* has indicated that there is evidence directly linking many learning disabilities to adverse reactions to childhood vaccines. In a June 2000 letter to members of the NVIC, Fisher wrote that the vaccine injury spectrum can include learning disabilities, ADHD, seizure disorders, mental retardation, asthma, diabetes, chronic fatigue, arthritis, inflammatory bowel syndrome, and other chronic diseases. In June 2000, the NVIC publicized this issue by sending *The Vaccine Reaction: Autism and Vaccines* to fifty-five thousand pediatricians, and all eight thousand members of Congress and state legislatures. For more information, contact the NVIC at 512 W. Maple Avenue, Suite #206, Vienna, VA 22180; (703) 938-0342; www.909shot.com.

Children with learning disabilities are protected by several federal and state regulations. Schools accepting monies from the government (i.e., public schools) are legally bound to adhere to these regulations. For more information regarding the laws and regulations that govern schools in your state, contact the Department of Education in the state in which you reside. If your child attends a private school, the regulations may differ from the public sector. This office will be able to answer your questions and provide the support you may need.

For more information about the disabilities mentioned here, along with others, please contact your local library or search the Web for support groups in your area. Here are a few books that may provide parents with a base of information:

- *Learning Disabilities A to Z: A Parent's Complete Guide to Learning Disabilities from Preschool to Adulthood* by Corinne Smith and Lisa Strick (New York: Free Press, 1997)

- *The Misunderstood Child: Understanding and Coping with Your Child's Learning Disabilities* by Larry B. Silver (New York: Times Books, 1998)
- *The ABC's of Learning Disabilities,* by Bernice Wong (New York: Academic Press, 1996)
- *Straight Talk about Reading: How Parents Can Make a Difference during the Early Years* (Chicago: Contemporary Books, 1999)
- *Learning to Read: A Call from Research to Action* (National Center for Learning Disabilities, 1997)
- *DPT: A Shot in the Dark* by Coulter and Fisher (Avery, 1991)

Modifying Behavior

Antsy behavior often gets in the way of learning for kids, hampering their chances for academic success. Their frustration level in turn will likely get them into trouble. Together, parents and the school can help such children before they get into *big* trouble.

Behavior modification is one option to parents, setting boundaries for children in a firm but friendly way. Parents often try these behavior modification programs first, before putting their hyperactive child on medication. The suggestions in this section will give examples for a behavior modification plan to help parents decide whether it is appropriate for their child. Let's take a look at some of the steps inherent in behavior modification:

- *Build confidence.* Parents may first want to try a positive approach, by building confidence. Focus on improvements, and notice contributions that the child is making around the house. Build on the child's strengths, and try to eliminate or extinguish the discussion about "bad" behavior. Children with behavior problems sometimes are seeking attention, and even negative attention rewards the negative behavior. So try turning it around by ignoring the things that you object to, and reward the behaviors that are rewarding to see. Show faith in your child; let her know you believe in her. When asking for a task to be done, limit the time allotted for the task, and acknowledge a task's difficulty.
- *While helping others, we often help ourselves.* Parents can help children focus their energy into activities in which they contribute

time and efforts. Many charity organizations are looking for young, energetic helpers. The local animal shelter, zoo, church, or soup kitchen would welcome a parent-and-child team to become involved. As parents, we lead by example. Show your child that you care, and provide this opportunity for the child to contribute by making a difference by helping others. Children are often centered around themselves, and with your help you could remind them of the feelings of others. Focus their high level of energy into promoting volunteerism and the rewards of helping those less fortunate.

- *Mistakes are okay.* When you have started to turn things around for you and your child, working together toward positive results with their behavior, talk about mistakes that may happen along the way. Equate mistakes with effort, and minimize the effects of the mistakes if you have seen some overall improvement. Remember that children are little people, waiting for their parents to "teach" them proper behavior by setting a good example. Be understanding and talk about changes or other alternatives for the future.

- *Teach responsibility.* Children can be responsible for small chores at an early age. A three-year-old can be responsible for wiping his or her mouth at the table. A five-year-old can put the napkins on the table for supper. An eleven-year-old child can set the table, put ice in the cups, and make a salad. A teen can help prepare the meal, with careful attention to the oven or stove. A young adult might even make the entire dinner. Children feel good about themselves when they contribute to the household's routine, and at the same time they're learning to be responsible members of their family.

- *Offering interventions/discipline.* When discussing a repeated mistake or a serious infraction, begin by clearly restating or defining the problem. Describe how you, the parent, feel about what was done. Ask the child how it made him feel. Insist that you have needs and that the family has needs that all members must respect. Discuss and evaluate a plan for solution. Develop a course of action that will involve the child, with you determining the effectiveness of the plan. Then a few weeks later, remember to mention how much you appreciate the child's efforts not to repeat the same mistake twice. This will reteach appropriate behavior and let the child know that you appreciate his efforts to be well behaved.

- *Set limits.* Children often test the boundaries that their parents set for them. As the parent, you have the right during an argument with the child to dodge irrelevant issues, take a time-out, impose a time-out on children, change the subject, refuse responsibility, state both viewpoints, table the discussion until later, or agree with the child. If you hand off the power to the child, then the child will be in control of you and the family. It is important to remember that each member of the family has rights, and no one person has the right to infringe on the others' rights routinely. Some parents can be manipulated by their children; others command respect by respecting the children, in accord with the old saying "You get what you give." Parents are not always in the right and should acknowledge when they make a mistake. This will allow the child to see that people can admit their mistakes and move past them. They will see that you are willing to work with them, by being a good example yourself.

These tips are only the beginning of behavior modification in the home. If they do not help, find an expert that can give you additional support. Your child's school might be a good starting point.

Some schools have behavior specialists who are hired to keep children on task and to redirect them to learning. These services may range from giving subtle hints to the child to physically removing the child from an area of the school if the child is not complying. Check with the school officials to inquire about the specific techniques approved for use in the school district. These behavior specialists need to have support of the parents, or the child will not progress as quickly.

Working together with the school as educational partners is the greatest investment of time that you can give to your child. Contact your child's school counselor or principal or the county children's services agency for information about behavior specialists serving your area. Classroom teachers can't do it without your help. If you feel that you are having difficulty communicating your child's needs to the school, a child advocate, who is trained in understanding emotions, can help you to express and communicate with strong feelings. Child advocates can be found in your local telephone book or through the local mental health agency, counseling agency, or children's services agency.

Children of today have not changed from the children of yesterday, but the choices they make have changed. Children chose to bring gum to school years ago, and they are choosing to bring weapons to school now. Parents can help their children make the right choices and learn from their mistakes, accepting them as the individuals they are. Love is a gift with no strings attached. Use every moment of every day as a learning experience with your child, and grow together as a team for positive change.

For more information on behavior modification techniques, refer to the following publications:

- *Parenting,* December 1987
- *Cooperative Discipline Implementation Guide* (Circle Pines, MN: American Guidance Service, 1995)
- *Bringing Home Cooperative Discipline* (Circle Pines, MN: American Guidance Service, 1995)
- *Responsible Kids in School and at Home* (Circle Pines, MN: American Guidance Service, 1994)
- *Coping with Kids,* by Linda Albert (Tampa, FL: Alkorn House, 1993)

Be Nice to the Principal

Many parents think of the principal only as the "complaint department": they go to the principal when there is a problem. They may have forgotten that the principal may be the only person who can help. The principal is charged with the sole responsibility of protecting the health, safety, and welfare of the children in the school. The teachers and other personnel get paid to do a specific job. It is the principal's job to ensure that they are doing their jobs effectively. The principal is usually a mandated reporter of child abuse and will always be looking out for the child's best interest. Some commonly asked questions that parents have are addressed in this chapter.

My child was in a fight. Now what?

It is best to become an active listener. Listen first to what the principal and/or teacher says. Do not interrupt, for you may miss a detail or bit of information that is important. Once you have heard their side, give your child a chance to explain and then compare the two versions of the same event. Meet face to face, if necessary, to investigate and clarify the differences in details regarding the same event.

Remember to review the student handbook *before* a fight breaks out, to be sure that your child understands the consequences of his actions ahead of time. The student handbook will list the disciplinary infractions and district-approved consequences for children who break the rules. This will help both you and your child to be sure that communication is flowing, and may ward off problems. Usually, for fighting both parties may be given a three- to ten-day suspension from school, regardless of who started the fight. If your child did nothing, then you must support him and find witnesses to attest to that fact. Your child has due process rights, including a right to tell his side of the story, at an informal hearing and even at a formal hearing if requested by parents. You may want to get more information before appealing the school administrator's decision. An attorney can advise you about the particulars of your case. This will only serve as a guide to continue to work with the school in your child's best interests.

If your child did indeed fight, encourage him to acknowledge the mistake, try to better control the emotions next time, and get over it quickly. There is nothing worse than carrying a grudge or allowing frustration to build and build. This onetime fight is over, and the child should not resent the teacher, principal, or others for his own actions. Consequences are part of growing up, and school is simply a community of learners who also are held accountable for their actions. School prepares children; it teaches them to become productive citizens. Some lessons of life are difficult to learn, but it is all part of the process of growing up as a responsible citizen in America.

My child is failing. How can I help her pass?

Parents often find out too late that their child is failing. They see the first report card and the progress grades. If the grades are failing, then a parent must take action immediately. In many schools, if a child fails half the year in major subject areas, she will then fail that particular grade level and need to repeat it all over again. A parent should become involved and stay involved at the first sign of failing grades on the report card. Sure, some students may receive a failing grade on a test and recover the overall grade by doing better on the next test with parental support and encouragement. However, if a child has a failing grade on the report card, it is time to visit the teacher. If you do not receive satisfaction from talking to the teacher about ways to help your child to pass, go to the principal next. Many different programs, agencies, and personnel are available to help, but you need to ask.

My child was hit by his teacher. Can you help?

In this case, the principal should be your first contact. You should meet in person about this situation. There is no reason for a teacher to hit a child, except in the performance of the teacher's duties—to quell a disturbance, stop a child from hurting himself or others, break up a fight, or administer corporal punishment (paddling for disciplinary purposes). Become an active listener, gathering information from the child and the school personnel. You may want to question the child about others who could serve as witnesses. The parents need to work with the principal, providing all information for the principal to investigate. Children are usually able to give an accurate account of the situation and usually will be truthful when questioned. You know your child and the signs of truthfulness or stress and thus can determine the veracity of the situation.

The principal then will usually confer with the superintendent of schools in dealing with the teacher. You may not learn about the discipline of the teacher, because it is very confidential. If you do not feel comfortable with the methods of the school, an attorney could represent you in these matters in a calm yet authoritative style.

My child can't read. What can I do?

Parents are their child's first teacher. We must set a good example by reading to our children and showing them the value of reading by reading the newspaper, magazines, and other materials at home. National standards for reading say that children should read independently alone by third grade. If your child cannot read to you and you identify problems in reading, contact the teacher, reading supervisor, and/or counselor first. If you are not able to find help to reteach, tutor, or strengthen reading skills, contact your child's principal. She will be impressed that you exhausted all other channels and will recognize you as a caring parent. The principal probably will refer you to those individuals first and then help you to find reading support for your child. Your child may also have a learning disability, in which case the principal can help with networking services as well.

How can I get more involved in my child's school?

Opportunities abound for a parent to become involved at school. Parents as partners is a big focus, especially in elementary schools. The idea of including parents as classroom volunteers and teacher helpers has also swept the nation in elementary, middle, junior high, and senior high schools. Parents and teachers working together will show the children that education counts! You can call the school's secretary to inquire about volunteering. Some teachers have special projects throughout the year (arts, crafts, cooking) and need parents to volunteer. Remember to be willing to help out in any way! Please don't approach the school with a certain job in mind. They know where your help is most needed and assuredly will appreciate all that you can do. Remember also that you are a guest in the school, and you must keep any information about the children, teachers, principal, and staff confidential. A volunteer who gossips about the school will most likely not be invited back again.

Someone stole my child's only jacket. Can you investigate?

Children from different cultures and socioeconomic backgrounds attend the same schools. This means that your child may have to deal with others wanting her belongings. Teachers often tell children to keep their valuables at home. Some schools have uniforms that all children wear, to deter the desire for theft. It is a good idea not to send valuables to school. School personnel are in the business of educating children. They are not guards of your child's belongings. Children who aren't responsible enough to take good care of their things should have parents monitor what they bring to school. When an important article of clothing such as a coat is stolen, the school personnel need to be contacted for help. Begin with an investigation by the teacher. Ask the teacher to help you to find your child's jacket. If you feel that the teacher is not interested or not able to help, then contact the principal. The principal may have an idea of where the jacket can be found. The principal probably knows about an area for the lost and found or may know of a child who was wearing a jacket similar to the missing jacket. The principal is able to see things from a schoolwide view and may have additional resources to help.

My child is being bullied for money. Can you help?

Additional help on this topic appears in the "Beware of Bullies" section of this book; however, remember that bullying for money is extortion. Children are governed by laws as well as the policies of the school. You should begin with speaking to your child's teacher, counselor, and lastly the principal. Give the school personnel a week to resolve the situation. If you do not receive comfort or satisfaction, you may want to contact other authorities. School administration will most often cooperate with the police, juvenile probation office, or an attorney to make your solution even easier to acquire. When people work together, things get done. Children should be the focus of conversations, and remember to ask for everyone to work together to help your child resolve this situation. It is the adults' responsibility to help youngsters through childhood. Social and emotional development is an important part of growing up healthy. Children need to feel secure in their environment, and they need our help to keep their environment safe at school and at home.

Normal Operations of the School

Parents can help with their school's normal operation in many ways through cooperation and communication. The contribution of time and patience is sometimes the best donation you can give the school. Many of the normal operations of the school are controlled by upper management and by the tax base of financial limitations. Normal operations of the school such as these are difficult to change:

- *Physical environment.* The school was inherited by the officials who made the decisions to build it that way. Unless it is new or newly renovated, there is no reason to complain about the physical building. There are ways to improve the learning environment for your child.
- *Lighting.* The classrooms should be well-lit areas, with appropriate level of intensity. Some schools have "natural" light, while others have fluorescent lighting. If you have a child who experiences migraine headaches or says that the lighting needs to be adjusted, contact the school nurse or principal to seek help.
- *Class size.* There are many benefits to a smaller class. The teacher has fewer students among which to divide her time, allowing more individualized instruction for every child. A federal initiative suggests a smaller number of students in each classroom. This Class Size Reduction Act has an impact on all public schools in America. The federal government has offered monies to districts to hire additional teachers in grades 1, 2, and 3 to reduce the number of children assigned to one particular teacher. Ideally the class size

should range between twenty and twenty-five students per class-room. You can check with your school district officials to inquire about this initiative, if your child is in a large class.

- *Classmates.* Some children are not able to get along well in school. If your child has a history of trouble with one or two children, ask the principal to keep this in mind when assigning your child to a class. This may reduce your child's anxieties about school, as well as help the school to stop problems before they start.
- *Social considerations.* Friends do not always remain together in the same class. It is difficult to ask the principal to assign your child with her friend, but you may want to try. If you do not get re-sults, then you can refer to the many suggestions mentioned earlier in "Choosing the Teacher."
- *Classroom design.* Classroom structure is important to your child. If she wears glasses, for example, and the desks are placed in rows, you could ask that your child be placed near the blackboard or up front near the teacher. If the desks are arranged in a U shape, you may want to be sure that your child's back is not facing the teacher all day. Tailor such suggestions to your child's needs.
- *Food served in the cafeteria.* Children who are lactose-intolerant or allergic to certain foods will need to be accommodated by the cafeteria staff with the help of the school nurse. Most children in school are able to eat everything the school provides. The school dietician plans a healthy, balanced meal providing nutrients that growing kids need. Encourage your child to eat at school by get-ting a monthly menu from the school and planning the days to-gether with your child. It may be difficult to pack a lunch that meets the same rigorous healthy components as those found in a school lunch.
- *Visitors' protocol.* Safe schools are everyone's responsibility. As a parent, please be understanding and patient with the guidelines set forth for visitors to the school. Visitors are usually asked to check in at the principal's office, and some schools may even secure a buzzer system that you need to press before entering the school doors.
- *Restricted areas to visitors.* Visitors are usually not able to roam the school. If you are visiting, check in at the administrator's of-

fice first. This may help to prevent your involvement in an embarrassing situation. You would not want visitors to be permitted around your child without purpose. You also would not want the school security or principal to escort you out of school for illegal entry. Protecting children is a job that the school takes seriously. Do your part to help out!

- *Confidential information.* Information about your child is restricted and considered confidential. If you suspect that confidential information is being passed among school officials, teachers, or staff, you should contact the school immediately. Parents must protect the safety of their children's reputation, because a bad reputation can be damaging to a child's self-esteem. Teachers may treat troublemakers differently, even before they get to know them. This different treatment in turn may be the cause of your child disliking school. Assure the school that they can come to you with problems and that you will expect the information to be kept confidential, as protected by law.

Progress Reports

Progress reports are a good way to keep track of your child's progress in school. Most schools provide these as an early warning notice for children who may be failing a particular grading period or for failing the year. Retention and promotion from grade to grade is a delicate thing. School personnel have a moral and ethical obligation to notify you that your child is failing and to allow you to participate with them as educational partners in helping the child succeed.

Progress reports should arrive in the middle of each progress period from your child's teacher or school office. This is the period between the issuance of report cards. Some schools send home report cards every six weeks, while others are every nine weeks. This information can be easily found in the student handbook that your child should receive near the beginning of each year. Some schools mail progress reports to your home, while others send them home for the child to give the parent. Parents should be alert to the arrival times of these reports. Talk to other parents to see whether their children have received progress reports in addition to the regular report card. Some students have been known to throw away the ones they are given at school and/or arrive first to the mail to intercept the progress letters to their parents. You may want to make routine calls to check with the school to see about your child's progress.

Retention/failure danger notices are an advanced and serious type of progress report. Failing a particular subject or grade level is no laughing matter, yet many young people do not take this seriously. A child who fails a particular subject in elementary school is more likely to recover this failure in the early grades. An older child who fails with retention of an entire grade level is at risk for dropping out of school later in high school. Retention can sometimes create a social barrier preventing your child from fitting in with his peers. Fitting into the third grade is not so much a problem as it is in eleventh grade, when teenagers begin to drive. If your child has failed a grade, he will most likely be one of few teenagers driving in tenth grade. This may not yet become a problem until his previous set of classmates graduates from high school, and your child has another year to attend in order to graduate. He may want to drop out of school at this point, at an age that parents have difficulty influencing their children.

Help your child pass! Retention and failure may be viewed as the final disastrous result, but there is much we can do as parents to prevent this from happening. Monitor your child's progress from elementary school through high school graduation. Become proactively involved in the education of your child. She should not feel ashamed to tell you that she is having trouble. Let your child know that if she is having trouble, you will help her find help. Discuss the value of education openly, and remember to be an active listener. We can learn a lot from and about our children by listening.

Progress reports may serve as a cue to request a tutor at school or inquire about programs designed to reteach skills. These tutors could be older children who are in the advanced classes or in the advanced placement program. In high school, teachers often have a period when they are available to help students in their classes. There may also be a list of teachers who will tutor children after school and/or in the summer months for a professional fee. Many charge $10 an hour, while others charge a rate decided on by their teachers' organization. You may want to take advantage of the tutoring programs that are offered free at school first and then later hire a tutor at your own expense. Children's own peers sometime make the best tutors because they can explain the lesson in terms that your child will better understand. If a child in the same class is passing and making good grades, that child would also make a very good tutor. Help your child learn the stuff she needs, thus giving her the power to make a passing grade.

Quick Tips

This section offers a variety of quick tips for working parents to make life easier yet enable them to help their child. Many working parents struggle for a balance, and these quick tips may help to provide more quality time for their children. For example, they may want to encourage their child to eat at school rather than packing their lunch each morning. This would save the parent valuable time before work and make the mornings less stressful for everyone. A parent may need to go to school one day to eat with their child. This will encourage the child to eat in the cafeteria, since children are usually afraid of changes. It would be worth the investment of time in the long run.

Parents may also want to find out whether their school has a school-sponsored breakfast program. Schools pay dieticians to provide well-balanced meals. Working parents could take advantage of these programs and at the same time unclutter their mornings. Parents may also want to check into after-school tutoring programs or after-school child care programs. These programs provide adult supervision and help with latchkey kids who come home to an empty home. Here are some other quick tips:

- *Car-pool children to school.* Working parents often look for short-cuts in getting their child to school. It may not always be possible to drive them to school personally, yet you probably do not want to leave your children home alone to catch the school bus. Consider beginning a car pool to school. One suggestion is to work it out with four other parents who have children in the same school.

Each parent could take one turn a week, keeping the children at their house until it was time to drive them to school. This could be a before-school activity, where they all eat breakfast together or watch a favorite show. This would then help by having a responsible adult with your child every morning. You could rotate the duties daily, weekly, or monthly. This organized plan may also help you to arrive at work on time four out of five mornings. The beauty in the plan comes with people who have the ability to be flexible with their schedule. If you can provide one day of service to your own child and four other children, you will benefit in having four days off from the morning commute.

- *Get an older child to help with homework.* This, as mentioned in the previous section, is the most practical way to get your child help with schoolwork. If you have an older child in the family who is able to help, your problems are solved. You may even know a neighbor child or a cousin who can help with lessons. As a parent, we can help until it begins to break down the relationships that we have with our child. Also, if someone else helps with homework, you are free to start supper or work on that report for the office. Help your child by getting homework help for him.

- *Pick out your child's clothes the night before.* This helps to reduce the amount of confusion in the morning and the number of last-minute decisions that need to be made. An organized plan helps as extra insurance that few things will unexpectedly happen to make you and your child late for school in the morning. Often parents tell me they have arguments in the morning about what their child is wearing to school. This then sends the child to school in an unhappy frame of mind. How can he do his best when he just had an argument with his parent? How can you expect him to learn if he feels silly or ugly in the clothes you made him wear? The feelings of children are as delicate as flowers. We must guide them and give them options to express their own individuality. Work it out the night before, to be sure that no misunderstandings arise.

- *Keep book bags, instruments, and notebooks in a special place.* Children regularly come to school unprepared and say that their book bag was in the car or that they did the homework but could not find their book in the morning. I then can only imagine the parent and child searching frantically before school for a book bag, clarinet, or notebook. Important items for school should have a special place. This will assure both you and your child can quickly find the materials to get ready for school. You may even want to put everything in the car the night before, so that it is ready for morning. It seems simple enough, yet it can help to make your morning routine more enjoyable with your child.

- *Be positive, and refrain from being critical before school.* Save the serious issues until after school, when you have time to work it out. Children need a good, healthy breakfast in the morning, and they need to connect emotionally with their parents to start the day in a good way. The things you do early will have a direct effect on the type of work your child does in school that day.

Ridicule and Teasing

The old saying "Sticks and stones will break my bones, but names will never hurt me" does *not* apply to children. Children can feel pain from the inside and the outside. Many of the shootings in American high schools had their beginnings in long-running ill feelings by the shooter because of ridicule and teasing. When children make fun of each other's differences, it hurts them. Here I will give examples of how ridicule can be reduced and the things a parent can do to counteract some of the effects of teasing or ridicule.

- *Name-calling/verbal abuse.* Name-calling is a difficult thing for children to endure, yet children do this as part of verbal abuse. Children should be discouraged from calling each other names. Parents can be a good example by refraining from this at home. You are your children's first teacher, and they learn well from you. If your child is being called names, you can help him cope with the name-caller by encouraging him to ignore it and also contacting your child's teacher, counselor, or principal.
- *Calling parents names.* Children also know that other children love their parents and so may call other parents by names to hurt the child. Encourage your child to ignore the names, and explain to them that their love for you is most important. Reinforce the idea that they do not have to take up a fight to defend your honor from name-callers. My own son attended my school and had to hear other children talking about me as the principal. I helped him cope by explaining that they do not know me as a person as well

as he does and that they are only upset at the role that I have in the school as disciplinarian. When he heard someone call me names, he often said, "You don't even know her very well" and would dismiss the comments. Find a way to help your child similarly dismiss the name-calling, and discourage them from fighting over a comment that is merely words.

- *Graffiti.* Sometimes children can be cruel by writing bad things on the bus stop, school building, or buildings seen along the way to school. This is horrifying when seen by the victim for the first time. Couple her own sad feelings with the feelings of humiliation from teasing and ridicule, and you could possibly have an explosive situation at school. If you see graffiti or you know of anything written along the path to school, contact the school principal immediately. Where there is gang activity, notification of graffiti helps officials to ward off problems before they start. Either way, graffiti hurts everyone, whether it affects your child directly or not. Demand that the school or local authorities remove the graffiti immediately. Schools should not be the battleground for settling disputes. Schools were designed to be learning institutions.

- *Inappropriate gestures.* Gestures are often the hardest to detect in the school system, because they are silent, yet they are just as offensive as vulgar language, name-calling, graffiti, and open ridicule. If your child tells you about gestures being given at school that mock or imitate some bodily harm, report it immediately as a threat to the school and officials. As mentioned in the section on gangs, gang members often use silent hand gestures as a form of communication. Be alert, and be aware!

- *Signs of depression.* Ridicule and teasing will sometimes wear down a kid to become depressed. Watch for the warning signs: withdrawal from family and other social activities, a sudden drop in academic performance, sullen and silent behavior, a change in clothing preferences, insomnia, a loss or increase in appetite, among others. The school does have professional personnel to help with depression, and they may recommend that your child visit a psychologist or psychiatrist. It is important that you get the child relief from depression, no matter where — school counselor, minister, therapist, or doctor. Depression, coupled with ridicule and teasing, can be a deadly mix. Help your child see her own worth and value. Make sure that she understands that you love her, and help shield her against ridicule or teasing. A child's self-esteem can be a greater predictor than intelligence for successes later in life, so continuously work to build a healthy self-esteem in your child.

Self-Esteem Building

How you express your love to your child tells him a great deal about himself. A child is a parent's treasure; however, parents may not always build their child's self-esteem to be as strong as it could be. There are many ways to enhance children's self-esteem. Teaching that mistakes are not "bad," for example, parents stress that mistakes are important for learning to be an adult. Loving your child also means respecting him as a person. Children need to be treated with respect and should receive unconditional love from parents. This message needs to be communicated while the children are both behaving and misbehaving.

Here are some ways parents can offer encouragement:

- Thank them, from age ten months and up: "Thanks for your cooperation!"
- Acknowledge their help: "I appreciate what you've done."
- Accept their concerns: "I can see your point."
- Differentiate between the child and the behavior: "I don't like what you just did."
- Give encouragement, which helps them reflect on their own personal value, rather than only pleasing their parents or authority figures: "You have done your best, and I am proud."

Parents also should avoid comparisons, celebrate and respect differences, and avoid competition between their children. Competition often results in children quitting because they cannot measure up. It also breeds conflict. Instead, teach them the joy of doing their personal best and the joy of doing instead of *out*doing someone else.

Let children feel valuable to you. Ask for their advice. Have them teach you something, such as how to play a game. Show them ways that they can be valuable to their siblings. Follow their lead in an activity of play. Concentrate on what they are doing well instead of dwelling on negative behavior. Respect and treat children as little people. For example:

- Respect their privacy and knock on their bedroom door before entering.
- Spend time with them when they are not misbehaving.
- Teach them that it is their responsibility to keep themselves encouraged.
- Don't nag or overparent.
- Give your child 100 percent of your focused attention and love.
- Negotiate how you will spend time together so you are both comfortable with the mutual decision.
- Share feelings that create closeness, caring, and love.
- Show unconditional love.
- Love them no matter what they do or do not do.
- Play, play, play with your child.

At times it is especially challenging to enhance self-esteem while modifying behaviors in children. Parents should remain calm, state the infraction, and avoid debating or arguing with the child. It helps to have preestablished consequences for misbehavior and avoid ridicule or hostile criticism. Remember the most important ingredient of parenting is to give unconditional love. Reward more than you punish, in order to be a main supporter of self-esteem. Praise immediately any and all good behaviors and performances. Find ways to encourage your child and encourage positive self-talk as well. For example, "You did very well remaining in your seat today. How do you feel about that?" Parents can encourage their children to think positively about themselves, thus enhancing their own perception of themselves.

Humiliation does not make children feel good about themselves. Get rid of the crazy idea that in order to make children do better, first you have to make them feel worse. Children are simply small adults, with the same feelings, hopes, and desires to be recognized as valuable people. Parents can be kind and firm at the same time. Try using positive reinforcement when reprimanding children, saying, for example, "You did not make your bed today. You did a fine job at it yesterday, but you need to try to remember every day."

Every effort must be made to discover ways for children to feel successful to themselves and appear confident to their classmates. America's schools are small communities that reflect the communities they serve. Positive parents promote positive schools.

Parent–Teacher Conferences

One of the most important times in your child's educational career is when you meet the teacher for a conference. Parents wait to be called by the school to address a concern or problem. Yet few parents take the proactive approach to meet the teacher *before* problems arise. Report cards, progress reports, and notes have their advantages, but the parent–teacher conference has the key ingredients. It is an opportunity for you to meet your child's teacher in person to discuss your child's educational progress in school.

You can begin with the assumption that each of you is interested in your child's happiness, health, and safety, as well as her academic successes. Schools want you to be interested because they need you to be involved. Each child's success at school depends greatly on the amount of support she receives from home. Good home–school relations are a must in every household. Research indicates that family involvement is the single most important factor in determining the success of children in school. Parent–teacher conferences are a good opportunity to share information and to become partners in your child's performance.

You can do many things to develop a working relationship with your child's teacher. First, let your child know that you will be meeting the teacher, and ask whether there is anything she would like you to discuss during the conference. This may prompt your child to share any "surprises," to prepare you before you get to school. Communication is the tool that makes the preconference, conference, and postconference a success.

BEFORE THE CONFERENCE

Before you go to school, make a list of questions that you and your family want to ask (homework, grades, attitude, behavior, strengths). You may want to ask your child these same questions and then compare these with the answers of the teacher during the conference. Some suggestions to begin with:

- What do you expect of my child?
- What do you expect my child to accomplish in your class? Do you feel that my child is working as well as she can be expected to work in your class?
- How much homework do you assign? Every day and weekends?
- Do you think my child enjoys your class?
- What kind of discipline in used in the class? How does my child react to this?
- When will my child's next report card be sent home? What grades should I expect to see?
- What special services or personnel are available to my child?
- What types of standardized tests are used in the school?
- What types of exams, projects, reports, and so forth, are required in your class?
- What information is kept in my child's permanent record file? Can I see it?
- Do you have any examples of my child's work in your class for me to review?
- Have you ever noticed any special interests or abilities in my child?
- Does my child get along with classmates?
- Does he show any leadership qualities?
- What about her participation in group activities?
- How can I become more involved in my child's education?

DURING THE CONFERENCE

It is important for you to be on time for your appointment. Begin the conference on a positive note, and offer a comment about something good that your child likes in the class. Next, refer to your list of prepared questions, so that you are able to stay on track. You do not want to get off track, without getting the information you need first. Ask the teacher about tests, exams, major projects, extra-credit opportunities, and on-line Internet support. Do not get nervous or worried if the teacher tells you something unexpected. Stay on track and continue with getting the answers to your questions. You don't have to memorize your list of questions; feel free to take out a written list to guide you during the conference.

Some teachers like to lead the conference, yet it is the parent who has come looking for answers. Teachers of today are forced to be in the customer service business of education. Remember that you and your child are the teacher's customers. The teacher shares the responsibility for educating your child. It is not a one-way process. Just as you expect satisfaction in a fast-food restaurant, you should achieve some sense of satisfaction in the fast-conference process. Your child is your treasure, and you can get some indication about her school-day successes by speaking to her teachers. You can stick to educational topics or move to discussing her peer group or friends. This is your opportunity to have a view of the inside, through the eyes of the teachers. Remember to be a good listener. You'll be surprised at how much you may learn by going to school as a parent.

Some teachers have Web sites, where parents can seek up-to-date information about their children's grades or upcoming projects. Ask the teacher to suggest ways for you to better support your child's learning at home. Listen carefully, and take notes to help you review the conference with your spouse, your child, or extended family members. If you run out of time, schedule another appointment in person, by telephone, or via e-mail.

AFTER THE CONFERENCE

Once you arrive home again, review the notes with your child and appropriate members of your family. It is not good to ridicule your child openly if the teacher did not have good things to report. Discuss how you, the teacher, and the child can work together to help your child do better in school. Stress the good things you learned at the conference.

Every child should hear at least one positive comment during the evening. Be careful not to alienate your child, and remind yourself that the goal of the conference was to help—not to hurt their feelings or damage their self-confidence. Low achievers may already feel inferior and sometimes feel special only in the eyes of their parents. Keep this relationship strong, and be prepared to help your child to succeed in school.

Make a plan together, and make it a high priority. Education is one thing that no one can take away from your child. It is a lifelong gift, and the quality time that you invest in your child will reap you a lifetime of rewards. Children need adults to respect their aspirations. They want parents to support them in their trials and tribulations and to celebrate their successes together. They need to have room for making mistakes and for excelling at whatever they try to do. They need parents to be good role models, who recognize the importance and value of a good education. They want you to get involved in their learning, by getting involved in their life.

Use What You Already Have at Home

Much of learning can be done using household utensils, with everyday tasks. Children are learning in many ways, throughout their day. As parents, including children in chores can be fun, if you include them in a loving, fun way, Here are some ideas:

- Folding towels involves fractions. You can easily explain folding the towel in half, thirds, and so forth. The child can truly understand the concept of fractions at an early age.
- Cooking recipes include many skills. You can talk about the importance of reading the recipe correctly, and explain units of measure and their abbreviations
- Chocolate pudding as finger paint is a fun way for preschoolers to learn to make letters. Alphabet cereal makes learning words fun, as you spell the word and have the child find the letters in the cereal bowl. Letter recognition and spelling of simple words will help your child to read more fluently later on.
- Measuring cups will encourage spatial understanding for small children. They enjoy putting each one into the other, while recognizing volume amounts. One-half cup is smaller than one cup, yet it holds more than one-third cup. Let the child experiment with these for greater understanding.

Children need more patience during their childhood than at any other time of their life. Every day offers learning experiences, and as adults, we sometimes forget this important point. They may make an honest mistake, and parents need to show understanding. When they are experiencing a growth spurt, their arm may be longer than it was a few days earlier. A child may honestly reach for a glass and spill it. This is frustrating to the child and to the parent who may overreact to the mistake. Plentiful patience and understanding should be given to children when they need it. We were all children, and we all know how it feels to make a mistake. Parents are entrusted with the responsibility of transforming mistakes into positive lessons, to prepare children to become young adults.

Violence and Drug Abuse in Our Schools

Why are schoolchildren using physical force to cause harm, damage, or abuse? What can parents do about their children attending school with abusive classmates? The former chief of the Office of National Drug Control Policy, General Barry McCaffrey, was quoted in the media urging parents to "Maintain your principles, and don't go into denial."

Violence in schools has recently been stemming from a higher than normal frustration level among peers. Although the risk of being killed at school is, literally, one in a million, according to the Centers for Disease Control (CDC), children are being confronted with the increasing threat of violence. A 1997 CDC survey reported that 8.5 percent of high school students carried a weapon on school property during the thirty days preceding the survey, and 7.4 percent of high school students were reported to have been threatened or injured with a weapon on school property during the twelve months preceding the survey.

According to a report by the National Center for Education Statistics, *Indicators of School Crime and Safety 2000* (U.S. Department of Education/U.S. Department of Justice), students ages twelve through eighteen were victims of more than 2.7 million total crimes at school during 1998. In that same year, there were also about 253,000 incidents of serious violent crimes at school (rape, sexual assault, robbery, and aggravated assault). There were sixty school-associated deaths in the United States between July 1, 1997, and June 30, 1998, including forty-seven homicides. In 1998, students were reported to be only twice as likely to be victims of serious violent crimes away from school as at school. The media also have reported issues of medication and depression in many of the school-age shooters who have made the headlines.

Parents sometimes suffer from a severe sense of denial in their children's early years. They often attack the school or the community without looking within their own child and his needs. The battles with school officials often conclude with parents seeking help from their doctor. Children are sometimes medicated to control their obsession with trouble. They may be put on antidepressants or a series of medications that help them to control their outbursts and not get in trouble as much. But what happens the day that they forget their medication, or they run out? This could be the day that the school has trouble. . . .

As a parent, how do you know when that day will be, and in which school? You don't, but you can help your child to stay out of harm's way through regular communication with the school. If your child is having behavior problems, ask about implementing a behavior modification plan to help your child, whether on medication or not. Reports indicate that approximately 50 percent of all classroom time is taken up with activities other than instruction, with discipline problems identified as responsible for the most significant portion of lost time.

Also reported by the National Center for Education Statistics in *Indicators of School Crime and Safety 2000* was that 13 percent of students ages twelve through eighteen reported that someone at school had used hate-related words against them during 1999. In other words, in the six months prior to the study, someone at school called them a derogatory word having to do with race/ethnicity, religion, disability, gender, or sexual orientation. In addition, 36 percent of students saw hate-related graffiti at school. These types of discipline problems can paralyze the entire learning environment for all children, not just a few.

Parents need to keep their *eyes wide open*, monitoring their child's activities as well as the activities of their child's friends. Research from the U.S. Department of Education indicates that within three years after leaving school, 70 percent of youth viewed as antisocial in school get arrested.

Many schools follow their state's crime codes in prosecution of drug abusers on school property. This means that counterfeit or look-alike substances are dealt with just like the real drug. Some officials feel that look-alike drugs are often sent into a school to "test" its drug policies and practices, before drug dealers bring the real drugs into an educational setting. School officials have a responsibility to protect the student population, and even counterfeit drugs jeopardize the safety of everyone.

According to McCaffrey, "Parents and adult mentors of children can make all the difference in the world. Kids are listening to you. If a person reaches age twenty without smoking, drinking, or using drugs, he or she is almost guaranteed to be drug-free for life."

Effective strategies used by parents and administrators to protect children are found in the following materials:

- Visit www.whitehousedrugpolicy.gov.
- For a free copy of "Growing Up Drug Free: A Parent's Guide to Prevention," write Consumer Information Center, Dept. 27, Pueblo, CO 81009.
- In the book *Children in Danger: Coping with the Consequences of Community Violence,* by J. Garbarino, N. Dubrow, K. Kostelny, and C. Pardo (San Francisco: Jossey-Bass, 1992), child development specialists look at the effects of growing up in the "war zones" of such cities as Los Angeles, Chicago, and Washington, D.C., and show how teachers, parents, social workers, and counselors can help "restore the child to childhood."
- *Everyone Wins! Cooperative Games and Activities,* by S. and J. Luvmour (Philadelphia: New Society, 1990), is an easy reference guide for teachers, family members, and group leaders. It offers more than 150 games and activities selected to help children resolve conflicts, enhance communication, build self-esteem, appreciate one another, and be creative.
- "I Can Problem Solve" is a program for preschool, primary, and intermediate grades that teaches children thinking skills that can be used to help resolve or prevent "people" problems.
- Contact the Stop the Violence Movement Clearinghouse, The National Urban League, Inc., 120 Wall Street, New York, NY 10005, for materials and audiovisual aids by celebrity artists.

Watch for Warning Signs

Bookstores are full of books describing the signs of problems in a child's life. Parents must work hard to make their home a happy, positive place. Parents are competing with video games and technological advancements for time with their children. Warning signs to look for when a child is in trouble may include the following:

- Isolation
- Restlessness or insomnia
- Excessive sleeping or depression
- A sudden, sharp decline in grades
- Obsession with death
- Crying or having nightmares
- Obsession with guns
- Sneaking out of the house
- Denial of religious affiliation
- Trouble with teachers in school
- Self-mutilation (cutting, burning, carving into one's skin)
- Mannerisms, signals, secretive phone calls
- Gang friends or a certain code of dress (e.g., dark clothing)
- Trouble at school

Educators and families can increase their ability to recognize early warning signs by establishing a close, supportive relationship with children by caring to know them well enough to be aware of their needs, feelings, attitudes, and behavior patterns. Educators and parents together can review school records for patterns of behavior or sudden changes in those behaviors.

In April 2000 the U.S. Departments of Education and Justice and the American Institutes for Research released *Safeguarding Our Children: An Action Guide,* by K. Dwyer and D. Osher. This book describes the following early warning signs. As parents, we must use these early warning signs responsibly. None of them alone is sufficient for predicting aggression or violence. Also, the early warning signs described here are not equally significant, and they are not presented in order of seriousness.

- *Social withdrawal.* In some situations, gradual and eventually complete withdrawal from social contacts can be an important indicator of a troubled child. Social withdrawal often stems from feelings of depression, rejection, persecution, unworthiness, and lack of confidence.
- *Excessive feelings of isolation and being alone.* Research has shown that the majority of children who are isolated and appear to be friendless are not violent. In fact, these feelings are sometimes characteristic of children who may be troubled or withdrawn or have internal issues that hinder development of social affiliations. However, research also has shown that in some cases, feelings of isolation and not having friends are associated with children who behave aggressively and violently.
- *Excessive feelings of rejection.* In the process of growing up and the trials of adolescent development, many young people experience emotionally painful rejection. Children who are troubled often are isolated from their mentally healthy peers. Their responses to rejection will depend on many background environmental factors. Without support, they may be at risk of expressing their emotional distress in negative ways, including violence. Some aggressive children who are rejected by nonaggressive peers reach out to aggressive friends who, in turn, reinforce their violent tendencies.
- *Being a victim of violence.* Children who are victims of violence— including physical or sexual abuse in the community, at school, or at home—are sometimes at risk themselves of becoming violent toward themselves or others.

- *Feelings of being picked on and persecuted.* The child who feels constantly picked on, teased, bullied, singled out for ridicule, and humiliated at home or at school may initially withdraw socially. If not given adequate support in addressing these feelings, some children may vent them in inappropriate ways, including possible aggression or violence.
- *Low school interest and poor academic performance.* Poor school achievement can be the result of many factors. It is important to consider whether there is a drastic change in performance and/or poor performance becomes a chronic condition that limits the child's capacity to learn. In some situations (such as when the low achiever feels frustrated, unworthy, chastised, and denigrated), aggressive behaviors may occur. It is important to assess the emotional and cognitive reasons for the academic performance change to determine the true nature of the problem.
- *Expression of violence in writings and drawings.* Children and young adults often express their thoughts, feelings, desires, and intentions in their drawings and in stories, poetry, and other written forms. Many children produce work about violent themes that for the most part is harmless, when taken in context. However, the overrepresentation of violence in writings and drawings that is directed at specific individuals (family members, peers, other adults), consistently over time, may signal emotional problems and the potential for violence. Because there is real danger in misdiagnosing such a sign, it is important to seek the guidance of the qualified professional—such as a school psychologist, counselor, or other mental health specialist—to determine its meaning.
- *Uncontrolled anger.* Anger that is expressed frequently and intensely in response to minor irritants may signal potential violent behavior toward self or others.
- *Patterns of impulsive and chronic hitting, intimidating, and bullying behaviors.* Children often engage in acts of shoving and mild aggression. However, some mildly aggressive behaviors such as constant hitting and bullying of others that occur early in children's lives, if left unattended, might later escalate into more serious behaviors.
- *History of discipline problems.* Chronic behavior and disciplinary problems both in school and at home may suggest that emotional

needs are not being met. These unmet needs may be manifested in acting-out and aggressive behaviors. These problems may set the stage for the child to violate the norms and rules, defy authority, disengage from school, and engage in aggressive behaviors with other children and adults.

- *History of violent and aggressive behavior.* Unless provided with supports and counseling, a child who has a history of aggressive or violent behavior is likely to repeat those behaviors. Aggressive and violent acts may be directed toward other individuals, be expressed in cruelty to animals, or include fire setting. Youth who show an early pattern of antisocial behavior frequently and across multiple settings are particularly at risk for future aggressive and antisocial behavior. Similarly, youth who engage in overt behaviors such as bullying, generalized aggression, and defiance and covert behaviors such as stealing, vandalism, lying, cheating, and fire setting are also at risk for more serious aggressive behavior. Research suggests that the age of onset may be a key factor in interpreting early warning signs. For example, children who engage in aggression and drug abuse at an early age (before twelve years old) are more likely to show violence later on than are children who begin such behavior at an older age. In the presence of such signs, it is important to review the child's history with behavioral experts and seek observations and insights.
- *Intolerance for differences and prejudicial attitudes.* All children have likes and dislikes. However, an intense prejudice toward others based on racial, ethnic, religious, age, language, gender, ability, disabilities, health problems, or physical appearance, when coupled with other factors, may lead to violent assaults against those who are perceived to be different.
- *Drug use and alcohol use.* Apart from being unhealthy behaviors, drug use and alcohol use reduce self-control and expose children and youth to violence, either as perpetrators or as victims, or both.
- *Affiliation with gangs.* Gangs that support antisocial values and behaviors such as extortion, intimidation, and acts of violence toward other students can cause fear and stress among other students. Youth who were influenced by these groups (those who emulate their behavior as well as those who become affiliated with them)

may adopt these values and act in violent or aggressive ways in certain situations. Gang-related violence and turf battles are common occurrences tied to the use of drugs that often result in injury and/or death.

- *Inappropriate access to, possession of, and use of firearms.* Children and youth who inappropriately possess or have access to firearms can have an increased risk for violence. Research shows that such youngsters also have a higher probability of becoming victims. Families can reduce inappropriate access and use by restricting, monitoring, and supervising children's access to firearms and other weapons. Children who have a history of aggression, impulsiveness, or other emotional problems should not have access to firearms and other weapons.

- *Serious threats of violence (also an imminent warning sign).* Idle threats are a common response to frustration. Alternatively, one of the most reliable indicators that a child is likely to commit a dangerous act toward self or others is a detailed and specific threat to use violence. Recent incidents across the country clearly indicate that threats to commit violence against oneself or others should be taken very seriously. Steps must be taken to understand the nature of these threats and to prevent them from being carried out.

Parents see these warning signs, yet sometimes it is difficult to act responsibly since they love their children. However, with society's low tolerance for violence in schools, children are facing very serious criminal charges from their actions. Yes, it may be difficult to express the "tough love" necessary to get your child the help he needs. However, as parents we are raising the children of today to become the adults of tomorrow. We have help: Agencies, counselors, school personnel, law enforcement agents, and others can provide assistance and support. Speak to these professionals, while responding to urgent messages or signs from the child.

Use the early warning signs to shape intervention practices. Working together with your child's school, a parent can be actively involved in shaping practices and policy. Adults in school communities can use their knowledge of early warning signs to address problems before they escalate into violence. An early warning sign is not always a predictor that a child will commit a violent act toward self or others.

Effective schools recognize the potential in every child to overcome difficult experiences to control negative emotions. They support staff, students, and families in understanding the early warning signs. School boards should have policies in place that support training and ongoing consultation to ensure that the entire school community knows how to identify early warning signs and understands the principles that support them.

Parents and school staff also must identify and respond to urgent warning signs. Unlike early warning signs, urgent warning signs indicate that a student is very close to behaving in a way that is potentially dangerous to self or others. These warning signs require an immediate response. No single warning sign can predict that a dangerous act will occur. Rather, imminent warning signs usually are presented as a sequence of overt, serious, hostile behaviors or threats directed at peers, staff, or other individuals. Usually, imminent warning signs are evident to more than one staff member, as well as to the child's family. Imminent warning signs may include the following:

- Serious physical fighting with peers or family members
- Severe destruction of property
- Severe rage for seemingly minor reasons
- Detailed threats of lethal violence
- Possession and/or use of firearms and other weapons
- Other self-injurious behaviors or threats of suicide

When warning signs indicate the danger is imminent, safety must *always* be the first and foremost consideration. Action *must* be taken immediately. Immediate intervention by parents and school authorities and possibly law enforcement officers is needed when a child has presented a detailed plan of the time, place, and method to harm or kill others, particularly if the child has a history of aggression or has attempted to carry out threats in the past *and/or* is carrying a weapon, particularly a firearm, and has threatened to use it.

The Gun Free Schools Act requires that each state receiving federal funds under the Elementary and Secondary Education Act (ESEA) must have put in effect, by October 1995, a state law requiring local educational agencies to expel from school (for a period of not less than one year) a student who is determined to have brought a firearm to school. Each state's law also must allow the chief administering officer of the local educational agency to modify the expulsion requirement on a case-by-case basis. All local educational agencies receiving ESEA funds must have a policy that requires the referral of any student who brings a firearm to school to the criminal justice or juvenile justice system.

School leaders are expected to encourage others to raise concerns about observed early warning signs and report all observations of imminent warning signs immediately. This recommendation is in addition to school district policies that sanction and promote the identification of early warning signs. Easy access to a team of specialists trained in evaluating and addressing serious behavioral and academic concerns is a necessity in today's schools. In many schools, the principal is the first point of contact. In cases that do not pose imminent danger, the principal contacts a school psychologist or other qualified professional, who then takes responsibility for addressing the concern immediately. If the concern is determined to be serious but not pose a threat of imminent danger, the child's family should be contacted. The family should always be consulted before implementing any interventions with the child.

It is often difficult to acknowledge that a child is troubled. Sharpen your skills as a parent and offer your child support, kindness, and a sense of order and purpose. The odds are that the better you meet these needs, the less your children will turn to gang activity, drugs, alcohol, and violence. Try these suggestions:

- Talk with your child and become an active listener.
- Try to understand the situation from your child's point of view, and explain your view in his terms.
- Have high expectations for learning, and value education. Do everything possible to prevent your children from dropping out of school. The school is a great resource and can be a watchful eye.
- Involve your child in positive group activities.
- Know where your child is and whom he is with at all times.
- Encourage your child to excel and succeed in school to the best of his abilities.

- Understand early and imminent warning signs when fostering a safe school and parent partnership. Become an active participant in your child's life at home, in the community, and at school.

The following resources offer more information on violence prevention:

- U.S. Department of Education: http://www.ed.gov/offices/OSERS/OSEP/earlywrn.html
- *Safeguarding Our Children: An Action Guide* (Washington, D.C.: U.S. Departments of Education and Justice, 2000)
- The National Congress of Parents and Teachers, Chicago IL 60611: documents on gangs and schools, and successful initiatives that have been implemented by local parent groups nationwide
- Bureau of Alcohol, Tobacco, and Firearms, United States Department of Treasury: (800) ATF-GUNS; a toll-free number for citizens to report illegal activity involving guns
- National School Safety Center, Westlake Village, CA 91362; (805) 373-9977: print resources on how to address problems of gangs and violence in a community or school setting
- National Crime Prevention Council, Washington, DC 20006: information on getting a neighborhood group organized for crime prevention
- National Association of Elementary School Principals, (703) 684-3345

Extra Help with the Internet

As discussed earlier, the Internet can be a helpful tool for children of all ages when used in the proper manner and supervised by responsible adults. Children can use the Internet for school projects, to connect with different parts of our global community, and to complete courses at home on-line. Many sites and Internet servers can help parents set precautions on their computer, thus protecting their children while on the Internet. Experts also suggest that children should not use their real name and should not ever reveal where they live or their scheduled daily activities on-line. We all have heard horror stories about dangerous adults who have invited children to meet them after first developing a friendship via the Internet. This is a new danger to parents of the twenty-first century that our own parents did not have to face.

For parents to take a proactive approach to helping their children on the Internet, we must provide children with developmentally appropriate sites to visit. They should be both fun and very interesting to kids. Here are some Internet locations that may interest both you and your child:

Library of Congress: http://lcweb2.loc.gov/frd/cs/cshome.html
Comparing Nations: http://www.your-nation.com
3D Atlas: http:www.3datlas.com
States of the nation: http://www.globalcomputing.com/states.html
Encyclopedia: http://www.encyclopedia.com
Olympics: http://www.olympic.org
U.S. Olympics: http://www.olympic-usa.org

Outdoor resorts: http://www.rsn.com
The NFL: http://www.nfl.com
All teams: http://www.netguide.com/guide/sports/nfl.html
Major League Baseball: http://www.majorleaguebaseball.com
Baseball hometown newspapers: http://www.purebaseball.com
The NHL: http://www.nhl.com
Golf: http://www.golf.com
Cybergolf: http://www.cybergolf.com
Ski information: http://www.alpworld.com
College sports fans: http://www.FANSonly.com
HBO boxing: http://www.hbo.com/boxing
Wrestlemania: http://wcwwrestling.com
Surfin' U.S.A.: http://www.surfermag.com
Running: http://www.runningonline.com
Bowling: http://www.pbatour.com
Chess: http://www.chessed.com
Billiards: http://www.billiardworld.com
NASCAR racing: http://www.nascar.com
Travel: http://www.4sportstravel.com
Museum U.S.A.: http://www.museumca.org/usa
Scholarship search: http://www.fastweb.com

Your Adolescent Child

It has been said that the most important things to adolescents are (1) their hair and (2) their friends. This is a difficult concept to comprehend when trying to reason with a thirteen-year-old, and this is why the other chapters of the book encourage parents to keep involved with their children at all stages of their life.

Preadolescence is usually identified as being between the ages of six and twelve years old, while adolescence ranges from twelve to eighteen. Preadolescence is the transition between childhood and true adolescence. During these years, it is often difficult to reason with your child, as she demands a reason for everything. As parents, we need to make some decisions based on intuition, and this is not easily explained to a youngster. Did you ever try to change the mind of an adult friend who completely disagrees with your viewpoint? This is an excellent example of the technique most likely to find success with your child. Approach the issues or concerns with guarded optimism, and be careful to not lose your sense of manners and patience when explaining your reasons. If you would not yell your opinion to your best friend, then you would most likely not yell it to your child. We need to give our loved ones as much respect as we do our friends. Be careful to foster an open-minded relationship, while teaching and guiding the child. As children grow up, they usually give what they get. If they are treated with disrespect as a child, they will likely give their parents disrespectful treatment and attitude during adolescence. If you slam the door shut, you have not met the child's needs or your own.

Most of my friends and parents whom I meet at school with teenagers marvel at their child's persistent nature. For example, one child wanted a dirt bike in June and kept asking every day for the bike, trying to wear his mother down to buy one for him. He called her at work, left notes on the table, woke her up at night, and was even willing to sell his football cards to raise money to buy the dirt bike. I was impressed by her strength and reasoning ability. She continued (unwaveringly) to explain that she was afraid that he would get hurt on the bike and that she loved him too much for him to get hurt. Then the next month, the same boy wanted eight hundred paintballs for his paintball gun, to go to a birthday party that had a paintball theme. This mother agreed to this request because she felt that it was reasonable. Then her son forgot all about the dirt bike, and she said that it was no longer an issue.

Another child wanted to play football, and his dad would not allow it because of his own injuries playing the sport. The child walked around in a depressed state, with a very poor attitude around the house, until the parents gave in. The boy went out for the football team; he hated having practice every night of the week because it interfered with the rest of his life, and he ultimately quit within a month! In this case, maybe the parents allowed the child to learn a lesson for himself.

Another girl wanted a trampoline in her backyard and kept asking her parents about it for nearly a month, until she verbally wore them down and they agreed. Then, it sat in the backyard and was only used when friends came to visit.

In each of these three examples, the teenagers were persistent, keeping up the same pitch for something for nearly a month. If you are experiencing the same pressures of parenthood, do not fret! Parenting a teenager means that you can still teach and guide them, while hoping for the best. It hard to know when to say no, but your instincts as a parent will help you know. Follow those instincts, and trust that you make the right decisions.

Another common trait found in adolescents is the ability to have selective hearing; that is, they are able to "tune out" what their parents are saying. They hear only what they consider important to their cause (dirt bike, paintballs, football, trampoline, etc.) and turn off listening to other stuff. To varying degrees, most parents are tuned out by their adolescents during those first attempts for independence. This is a very uncomfortable but common experience for parents.

Parents who are ignored the most are those who from day one have not consistently taught their children to listen and respect them. The early years have a *big* impact on the emergent adolescent. If parents have permitted their parental authority to be diminished over the years by a rebellious youngster, it is difficult for the parent to take control during adolescence. The youngster will not appreciate, agree to, or understand a new assertive parenting approach. This should not surprise you! If for more than ten years the child has grown up dictating for everyone at home, he will not willingly step down from the throne of authority. The child may likely accuse you of dictating and unloving, and the child may become even more disrespectful, unmanageable, and determined to test your rules. Remember that the insults and child's obsessions will fade, and you will finally regain your authority as the adult and, most important, as the parent.

Again, the early years are crucial, and the earlier in the child's life that you gain control, the easier it may be. This is often forgotten by parents, who think their disobedient youngster is cute when she uses swear words or acts like an adult at home. Yet, this situation often brings a heavy consequence, including many household arguments when the youngster becomes an adolescent. You have many years to mold your child's character. Seize the moment, and work on regaining the authority with loving reactions, long conversations, and patience in every learned lesson of life. Remember, our children are our treasure!

An adolescent child reminds me of a flower about to bloom. The roots begin early in life and are nurtured until it grows. Your adolescent may seem like a flower waiting to blossom, and he needs your help to become the best person that he is capable of becoming. Much of what you taught him in the elementary grades will carry him through the middle school years. The more positive information that you enter into his young heart, the more he has to draw from when looking to unanswered questions.

Your decisions directly affect the type of person your child becomes. As adults, it is our responsibility to make the world a better place by teaching our children to become responsible. You are teach-

ing them today how to become parents of their own children some-
day. Many child development specialists say that to become good at
parenting, you must have grown up with at least one positive role
model. Be that positive role model in your child's life so she can pass
it on for generations to come.

Zip, Zap, and Zeal!

These three little words say it all! From the first time you hold your newborn baby in your arms until the day your child embarks on his own, you will need zip, zap, and zeal to meet everyday challenges and reap the rewards for your child's greater benefit. I would like to share the synonyms of these three words to underscore their meaning:

Zip: vigor, vim, energy, vitality, spirit, animation, provocativeness
Zap: drive, vim, pep, determination
Zeal: fervor, eagerness, passion, fervency, vehemence, devotion, intensity, excitement, earnestness, inspiration, warmth, ardor, fanaticism, enthusiasm

Parenting is a rewarding job, when all things are going well. When life turns up the pressure, then parenting can sometimes seem like a chore. When you consider that your efforts and years of dedication to this little human being actually will make a difference in the world, your zip, zap, and zeal will reap a lifetime of rewards.

Children are our greatest resource and our greatest treasure. Some people think of children as a *tabula rasa,* meaning a blank slate on which we can write our feelings, hopes, dreams, and character. If you have been blessed with this miracle of having a child to care for and love, you already know in your heart the importance of your role. Parents can no longer stay on the sidelines and watch as their children grow up. Parents need to bring the zip, zap, and zeal that they have to spark our public schools proactively. Become a partner in your child's education. Take an active part in molding a child's future. Invest in the future. Spend your time with children. The time to enjoy your child is *now*!

Conclusion

Every parent wants their child to go to school in a safe place, focused on teaching and learning. Many parents wonder about schools and want to know what is going on inside their child's school. *Children First: ABCs of School Success* has provided you with helpful hints about different situations that children experience and offers solutions for success in school. This book can help parents help their children by becoming an educational partner with their school.

You have just read the topics ranging from A to Z, and I hope that you feel stronger in your role as a positive parent and better prepared to teach your children ways to deal with some of the issues of the twenty-first century. Parenting today is not the same as it was a decade ago. Parents are faced with new challenges as they guide their children from infancy to adulthood. With this book, I hope that you have gained ideas to resolve conflicts, prevent violence, prepare your child for dealing with peer pressure, while strengthening academics in kindergarten through high school. It is meant to be a comprehensive guide covering a wide range of topics, putting children first and at the heart of all communications and home–school connections.

The book's many suggestions can wrap around your child like a security blanket during the school years. Many of the ideas here included after-school activities that will spark your child's interests and provide quality time for you and your child to share. In utilizing what you already have, you can learn and grow together, in everyday activities. Please take these ideas and expand them to fit your family's likes and needs.

Most of the ideas here focus on long-term solutions for success. These include ideas for behavioral support and positive parenting strategies. As an educator, I have heard many parents indicate that they want to steer their children away from trouble, yet they need to know the dangers of peer pressure, hidden dangers of the Internet, repercussions of personality conflicts between peers, and concerns about social activity. This is probably a parent's most challenging role, yet it can also be very rewarding. School personnel agree that children need their parents' support to guide them toward positive behavior and related activities. A good, solid education is one gift that you can help give your child that no other person can ever take away. The ability to read, for example, is a skill that can help your child reach great heights in school. A young adult with strong reading skills can achieve success, rather than getting in trouble.

Children First: ABCs of School Success was designed to help parents feel more comfortable in their child's school, by offering ideas that work. We want our children and students to be successful in school, resulting in a productive adult life. After all, the children of today will become the leaders of tomorrow.

About the Author

Shirley Babilya Dickinson is an educator, administrator, and child advocate. She has served sixteen years in the field of education, beginning as a teacher, and has been a principal for the past eight years. She has certifications in the areas of both elementary and secondary principalship, as well as her doctorate in education. She is also the mother of a school-age child.

Dr. Dickinson has published articles for the *PA Administrator*, *PA Association of Supervision & Curriculum Development's Best Practices in Southwestern PA*, and *PA Elementary and Secondary Principal's Newsletter*. She was an editor/writer for Apple Computer, Inc., in Pittsburgh and the *Focus Ed Newsletter* from 1987 to 1992. She presented at the 1999 PA Middle Schools Association Conference, the 1999 PA Elementary and Secondary Principal's Conference, and the 2000 National Middle School Association Conference in St. Louis. She is also an advocate for children as a member of the Greene County Covering Kids Coalition, which helps provide health coverage, and was recently appointed a member of Pennsylvania Partners for Children and the Advocacy Institute.

As a school principal and author, Dr. Dickinson has a burning desire to help children and their parents deal with current issues facing public schools.